Set design by Neil Patel

Photo by Richard Feldman

A scene from the Williamstown Theatre Festival production of *God of Vengeance*.

GOD OF VENGEANCE

BY DONALD MARGULIES

ADAPTED FROM THE PLAY BY
SHOLOM ASCH

BASED ON A LITERAL TRANSLATION BY
JOACHIM NEUGROSCHEL

★

DRAMATISTS
PLAY SERVICE
INC.

GOD OF VENGEANCE
Copyright © 2003, Donald Margulies

All Rights Reserved

SPECIAL NOTE

GOD OF VENGEANCE
by Donald Margulies
Adapted from the Play by Sholom Asch
Based on a Literal Translation by Joachim Neugroschel

The following acknowledgment must appear on the title page in all programs distributed in connection with performances of the Play:

God of Vengeance was originally produced by
A Contemporary Theatre, Seattle, Washington,
Gordon Edelstein, Artistic Director.

God of Vengeance was produced August 2002
by the Williamstown Theatre Festival,
Michael Ritchie, Producer.

Donald Margulies' version of GOD OF VENGEANCE received its world premiere at A Contemporary Theatre (Gordon Edelstein, Artistic Director; Jim Loder, Managing Director; Vito Zingarelli, Producing Director) in Seattle, Washington, on April 13, 2000. It was directed by Gordon Edelstein; the set design was by Hugh Landwehr; the lighting design was by Robert Wierzel; the original music and sound design were by John Gromada; the costume design was by Anna Oliver; the dramaturg was Liz Engelman; the dialect coach was Juli Rosenzweig; the fight director was Geoffrey Alm; and the stage manager was Anne Kearson. The cast was as follows:

JACK CHAPMAN .... Matthew Boston
SARA .... Nike Doukas
RIVKELE .... Rachel Miner
MANKE .... Naama Potok
HINDL .... Johanna Melamed
SHLOYME .... Mikael Salazar
REYZL .... Betsy Schwartz
BASHA .... Tricia Rodley
REB ELI .... Larry Block
THE SCRIBE (REB AARON) .... Sol Frieder
AN ORTHODOX MAN .... Andrew Traister
LOWER EAST SIDE KIDS .... Ian Nelson-Roehl, Scott Ross
THE PROSPECTIVE IN-LAW .... Wauchor Stephens
INDIGENTS .... Frank Krasnowsky, Jay A. Hurwitz
POOR WOMEN .... Ilene Fins, Hinda Kipnis
PARTYGOERS, MINYAN .... Mike Christensen, Matt Purvis,
                                                           Joe Shapiro, Mary Unruh

GOD OF VENGEANCE was subsequently produced by the Williamstown Theatre Festival (Michael Ritchie, Producer; Jenny C. Gersten, Associate Producer; Deborah Fehr, General Manager) in Williamstown, Massachusetts, on July 21, 2002. It was directed by Gordon Edelstein; the set design was by Neil Patel; the lighting design was by Rui Rita; the original music and sound design were by John Gromada; the costume design was by Candice Donnelly; the production manager was Christopher Akins; and the stage manager was Kelley Kirkpatrick. The cast was as follows:

JACK CHAPMAN .... Ron Liebman
SARA .... Diane Venora
RIVKELE .... Laura Breckenridge
MANKE .... Marin Hinkle
HINDL .... Jenny Bacon
SHLOYME .... Bruce MacVittie
REYZL .... Jenn Lee Harris
BASHA .... Christy Meyer
REB ELI .... Larry Block
THE SCRIBE (REB AARON) .... Sol Frieder
AN ORTHODOX MAN .... Joel Rooks
IRISH KID .... Michael Jerrod Moore
KID #2 .... Aaron Paternoster
THE PROSPECTIVE IN-LAW .... Mort Broch
INDIGENT #1 .... Daniel Deferrari
INDIGENT #2 .... Lee Rosen
POOR WOMAN #1 .... Rosalind Cramer
POOR WOMAN #2 .... Joyce Lazarus
POOR PEOPLE/PARTYGOERS ... Sarah Bellows, Nancy Burstein,
                                Natalie Jacobon, Melissa Miller,
                                Noam Rubin, Eric Neher
POOR PEOPLE/MINYAN .... Cy Beer, Robert James,
                            Michael Lively, Constantine Maroulis,
                                Eric Neher, Ben Russo,
                            Benjamin Strands, Mark Weimer

CHARACTERS

JACK CHAPMAN
SARA
RIVKELE
MANKE
HINDL
SHLOYME
REYZL
BASHA
REB ELI
THE SCRIBE (REB AARON)
AN ORTHODOX MAN
IRISH KID
KID #2
THE PROSPECTIVE IN-LAW
A HOMELESS MAN *
POOR WOMAN #1
POOR WOMAN #2
POOR PEOPLE
PARTYGOERS
MINYAN

PLACE

The Lower East Side of New York.

TIME

1923.

* Formerly two indigents.

GOD OF VENGEANCE

ACT ONE

The set consists of a two-story cross-section of a tenement building, the suggestion of an alleyway, a sidewalk, and a stoop. The tall buildings of the city loom in the background. The upstairs apartment is living quarters to Jack Chapman a.k.a. Yankel Tshaptshovitsh, his wife, Sara, and their daughter, Rivkele. The kitchen and master bedroom are not visible but the living/dining room and Rivkele's girlish bedroom are. The living room, decorated with framed family photos and a variety of tchotchkes, is an incongruous mix of Old World quaintness and greenhorn pretension. A fire escape is the urban balcony outside Rivkele's window, with a ladder that leads to the alley.

Downstairs, below the staid residence, is a brothel. Brass beds are partly concealed in cubicles behind exotic curtains. A chaise splashed with colorful fabrics is prominently placed in the main reception area. Washstand, liquor stash, Victrola, lamps, secondhand chairs. The walls are decorated with mismatched ornate mirrors and various pictures of women in seductive poses.

A collage of sounds of the teeming city. Lights up: a spring afternoon. We find Rivkele, seventeen years old, sitting forlornly at her window, like a jazz-age Rapunzel, humming a Yiddish song while embroidering a vestment.

*Manke, a streetwalker in her twenties, walks on and fixes her
lipstick while looking in a compact. An Orthodox man of late
middle-age nervously shields his face as he walks past, but not
without noticing Manke. Manke, standing near the stoop,
lights a cigarette. Sara comes on, her basket full of challahs
and flowers.*

SARA. *(To Manke.)* Move. *(Manke blows smoke in Sara's face and
giggles.)* Very funny. *(Sara goes upstairs, where she puts the flowers in
a vase and putters around the living room, sets a buffet table, etc.
Rivkele sees Manke from her window. Her face brightens. She calls in
a whisper:)*
RIVKELE. Manke! *(Manke's face loses its hardness when she sees her.)*
MANKE. Rivkele!
RIVKELE. I prayed you'd be there. I said, Please, God, I'm going
to look out my window, please let Manke be there. And you were!
MANKE. Shh shh shh.
RIVKELE. Look at my stitching. See? I'm doing as you said. *(She
shows her the vestment.)*
MANKE. It looks beautiful.
RIVKELE. I want to see you so much.
MANKE. Me, too. Come down!
RIVKELE. I can't. My father's having a party. And I'm the guest
of honor. *(The Orthodox man returns and nervously makes his move;
he clears his throat to get Manke's attention.)*
ORTHODOX MAN. Can we go somewhere?
MANKE. Yeah, sure. Right this way. *(She takes a final puff and
grinds out the cigarette, then blows a kiss to Rivkele and whispers.)* See
you later. *(Rivkele nods ruefully and waves as Manke leads the man
into the downstairs apartment. He warily follows, kissing the
mezuzah on his way in.)*
ORTHODOX MAN. So this is what it looks like.
MANKE. You were expecting the Waldorf-Astoria?
ORTHODOX MAN. You hear about such a place your whole
life … your imagination …
MANKE. It's just a place. Four walls, beds that sag in the middle.
My bed is here. *(She pulls open the drape on her cubicle and steps out*

of her dress.)

ORTHODOX MAN. No no no. Not so fast. *(A beat.)* Could we maybe talk a little first?

MANKE. Talk?

ORTHODOX MAN. Yeah. You know.

MANKE. We didn't come here for conversation.

ORTHODOX MAN. I know. But, please. Let's sit a minute. *(He sits down on the chaise. She shrugs, then sits next to him. Silence.)*

MANKE. *Nu? [Well...?]*

ORTHODOX MAN. I walked down this street so many times. Summer, winter. Went out of my way. Just to see you.

MANKE. You gawk at me, go home, screw your wife?

ORTHODOX MAN. No. *(A beat.)* I just got up from shiva.

MANKE. Oh. I'm sorry.

ORTHODOX MAN. *(Nods his thanks.)* She was sick a long time, my wife, may she rest in peace. A long time. *(Manke nods. Silence. He sighs deeply, inhales her aroma.)* What is that?

MANKE. Rose water. I dab some on my neck. *(She lifts her hair so he can smell her neck. He nearly swoons, gets up, moves away.)* What.

ORTHODOX MAN. I never should've come.

MANKE. Why not?

ORTHODOX MAN. It's a sin! What goes on here are sinful things! *(She laughs.)* What's so funny?

MANKE. Sin now, atone later. That's what they all do. *(Her laughter subsides. He's charmed.)*

ORTHODOX MAN. What's your name?

MANKE. Manke.

ORTHODOX MAN. Manke?! Is that so? I knew a girl named Manke, once.

MANKE. Yeah, yeah, I've heard that one before.

ORTHODOX MAN. No, I did. In the old country. Back in Vilna.

MANKE. Vilna?! You're from Vilna?

ORTHODOX MAN. Yes.

MANKE. I'm from Vilkia.

ORTHODOX MAN. Vilkia! Small world! My mother was born in Vilkia. Her name was Zide.

MANKE. *(Can't recall, shrugs.)* I left a long time ago. I was only seven.

ORTHODOX MAN. A child.

MANKE. Once.

ORTHODOX MAN. You're still a child.

MANKE. No. Not anymore. Not for a long time.

ORTHODOX MAN. Oh, but you are. Look at that *punim*. How does a girl with a face like an angel end up doing something like this?

MANKE. *(Brusquely gets up.)* Look, I don't want to talk anymore. Okay? No more talking. Talking's never a good idea. I wanna dance.

ORTHODOX MAN. Dance? *(She goes to the Victrola, puts on a jaunty Tin Pan Alley tune.)*

MANKE. There! Come on, let's dance! *(She pulls him to his feet. He resists.)*

ORTHODOX MAN. No, no, I can't …

MANKE. What do you mean, you can't?

ORTHODOX MAN. It's not allowed …

MANKE. You'll pay to *shtup* me but you won't dance with me? *(She snatches his hat and puts it on her head and teasingly dances around him.)*

ORTHODOX MAN. Hey! What are you doing?! You mustn't do that! Give it back! *(She gets him to move with her, awkwardly, in a dance-like way. He succumbs to her charms in spite of himself. Manke takes off the man's jacket, revealing his traditional garb underneath, and dons the jacket herself. She performs a seductive, sexually charged dance. Meanwhile, upstairs, Rivkele hears the music and dances freely, almost erotically, around her room. Wrapped in a paper-flower chain, her romantic reverie is shattered by her mother's call. Sara is putting on an apron.)*

SARA. Rivka! Rivkele, what are you doing in there? The whole house is shaking! *(Rivkele, breathless, stands guiltily in her doorway.)*

RIVKELE. Nothing.

SARA. Well, come. Finish with the decorations. *(Sara continues bustling about. Rivkele drapes paper flowers around the room. Downstairs: Manke's dance with the man has become more sultry. Trembling, he kisses her face. She turns off the music and, her back to him, walks to her cubicle and waits at the curtain. He braces himself and follows her in.)*

ORTHODOX MAN. *Oy gevalt. (As in, "What am I doing?" As the*

10

man sits on the bed and begins to remove his shoes, Manke looks at her watch, then draws the drape. Upstairs: Rivkele and Sara continue their preparations.)

RIVKELE. *(At the mirror.)* Look, Mama. Look how pretty it looks.

SARA. Yes, yes, very pretty. Stop dreaming. We want to be finished by the time your father gets home. Here, set these out. *(She gives Rivkele breads, etc., which the girl arranges.)*

RIVKELE. Will there be music at this party?

SARA. Music? What kind of music?

RIVKELE. I don't know, a little Sophie Tucker, maybe?

SARA. Sophie Tucker?! Your father wants to impress the men from the synagogue; all he would need is Sophie Tucker! He invites the whole neighborhood, practically, your father. If everyone comes who's invited ... I should've rolled up my rugs.

RIVKELE. Will girls be coming, too?

SARA. Girls? Maybe. Some people might bring their daughters. Nice Jewish girls.

RIVKELE. Will the girls from downstairs be coming?

SARA. *(Stops puttering.)* The girls from downstairs? What do you think? *(Resumes puttering. During the above, two hookers, Basha and Reyzl, both barely in their twenties, enter with two east side kids, one of whom is more confident than the other, who lags behind. They go into the brothel.)*

IRISH KID. *(Coaxing his reluctant friend.)* Come on!

BASHA. You boys sure you want to go through with this?

IRISH KID. Sure we're sure.

BASHA. 'Cause you don't have to.

IRISH KID. We're sure, we're sure.

REYZL. *(To Basha.)* Look how cute, they could be our kid brothers.

IRISH KID. Hey! We ain't your kid brothers.

REYZL. *(Feigns being impressed.)* Oh, well, pardon me!

IRISH KID. We been with plenty of girls.

BASHA. Okay, Casanova, who gets who?

IRISH KID. I'll take you.

BASHA. That okay with your friend?

IRISH KID. He don't care.

BASHA. Oh. Okay. *(Starts to lead him inside.)*

REYZL. *(To Kid Two.)* Well...? You coming, or what?

11

KID TWO. *(Takes a step, then backs away.)* Uh, I forgot, there's something I gotta do ... See ya, Francis ... *(He runs down the street.)*
BASHA. *(Teasing.)* "Francis"?
REYZL. *(Overlap, as Kid Two goes.)* What's the matter, you don't like my looks?!
IRISH KID. Ah, don't mind him. He's chicken. Hey, why don't you come, too?
REYZL. What do you mean?
IRISH KID. You know. You, me, and her.
REYZL. That's a new one, huh, Basha?
BASHA. It's gonna cost you double.
IRISH KID. I don't care. Moron gave me his money. *(Reyzl and Basha giggle as the threesome enter a cubicle and close the drape. Upstairs:)*
RIVKELE. What about dancing, Mama? Will there be dancing?
SARA. I said I didn't know if there was gonna be *music*.
RIVKELE. Oh, I hope so. I hope there is dancing. There's never any music in this house. Or dancing. I love to dance. I wish I had a silk dress and elegant, ladylike shoes to dance in, not these clumsy old schoolgirl shoes.
SARA. You wear schoolgirl shoes, my dear, because you are a girl! I hate to break it to you!
RIVKELE. But I'm not! I'm seventeen! Papa makes me wear these silly little dresses.
SARA. Don't let your father hear you talk like that. He takes such pride in you!
RIVKELE. Pride?! Like for a puppy, yes. Or a doll. For him to dress up and do with as he pleases.
SARA. Let me tell you something, darling. Your father may be smart about a lot of things but about women...? *(She shakes her head.)* Let me give you a little advice: Take what you can get from him. That's what I do.
RIVKELE. If only I could have some new clothes. Like I see in *Harper's Magazine*.
SARA. Well, once you're married, young lady — God willing, come Shevuas — you'll be free to dress ... however your husband sees fit.
RIVKELE. But I'm grown up already.

SARA. You're hardly grown up.

RIVKELE. Look at me, Mama.

SARA. Yeah, yeah, very nice.

RIVKELE. Stop what you're doing and look at me. *(She makes Sara stop and actually look at her.)* I am not a child. Am I.

SARA. *(A realization.)* No; you're not.

RIVKELE. *(Pinches her shirtwaist.)* See? I have breasts. And a waist. Manke says —

SARA. Manke!

RIVKELE. Manke says I have a very nice shape.

SARA. Oh, she does.

RIVKELE. She has all these beautiful clothes she says she'd let me wear.

SARA. Oh, really? I've got news for you: You're not putting on any of Manke's clothes.

RIVKELE. You should see, her closet is filled with — ! *(Stops herself.)*

SARA. Her closet? What do you know from Manke's closet?

RIVKELE. *(A confession.)* I've been down there.

SARA. Is that so?

RIVKELE. She's been teaching me how to embroider. Remember you said it would be good for me to learn?

SARA. I didn't mean for you to go down there!

RIVKELE. Then how, Mama, how was I to learn? She's taught me a lot. Wait, let me show you. *(She goes to her room to get the embroidered vestment.)*

SARA. *(Calls.)* You know the rules. If your father ever found out!

RIVKELE. *(Returns with the vestment.)* See? She's such a good teacher. See how well she draws? She drew the Star of David and the olive leaves. Just like the vestment in synagogue.

SARA. Manke did this?

RIVKELE. Yes. Isn't it beautiful?

SARA. He'll have a fit.

RIVKELE. I thought it would please him.

SARA. Please him?! It wouldn't please him — that you were getting embroidery lessons downstairs from Manke?! That her dirty hands touched something as sacred as this?!

RIVKELE. *(Over " ... something as sacred ... ")* Dirty hands? No,

Manke's hands aren't dirty. She's my friend.

SARA. Your "friend." Well, he doesn't want you mixing with the girls downstairs — and that's all there is to it. *(Downstairs, the Irish kid, wearing only his underwear and holding his clothes in a bundle, comes out of the cubicle and hurriedly gets into his clothes. Basha, wrapped in a sheet, and Reyzl follow.)*

BASHA. That was fast.

REYZL. I never even got my turn.

BASHA. What's the matter, "Francis"? Got a train to catch? *(The girls laugh derisively.)*

IRISH KID. Screw you.

BASHA. You wish. *(He starts to go.)*

REYZL. Hey, where you going? Pay up! *(Jack Chapman comes down the street with a bounce in his step.)*

BASHA. Hey! Mister! Stop him!

REYZL. He didn't pay! He owes us both!

JACK. *(Stops him, roughs him up.)* Oh, is that so? Trying to get a free ride, huh? Huh?

IRISH KID. *(Overlap.)* Hey! Leave me alone! Let go of me!

JACK. Nobody gets a free ride. You understand? Nobody!

IRISH KID. Get offa me — kike!

JACK. *(More incensed.)* Why you little *pisher!* Who do you think you are? Huh?! Pay up! You hear me? Hand it over! Before I wring your pimply little neck!

IRISH KID. *(Overlap.)* Here! Take it! Here's your stinking money! *(The kid crumples the money and tosses it to the ground.)*

JACK. Good! Now get the hell outta here! Go! *(He pushes the kid, who runs away. He shouts after him.)* And don't show your little Irish putz around here again! *Shaygetz!* *(He picks up the bills and smooths them out. To the girls.)* What are you looking at? *(They remain silent. He gives them each a dollar and puts the rest in his billfold. He changes his mind and gives them more.)* All right, now go fix yourselves up. Go on. *(Jack putters downstairs while Reyzl and Basha get dressed, fix their makeup. Meanwhile, upstairs:)*

RIVKELE. Does Papa really think I don't know what goes on down there? When I was old enough to ask questions, you know what he told me? He said it was a boardinghouse down there! A boardinghouse!

SARA. Never mind, you! Everything that man has done — good or bad — he's done for you. Don't you forget that.

RIVKELE. I know, Mama. *(Reyzl and Basha reemerge; Jack eggs them on; the girls go.)*

JACK. The night is young. Go go go!

SARA. He's trying so hard to change his ways. Give him a little credit, will you? *(Hears him coming up the stairs.)* Shhh. Here he comes. Be a good girl. It costs a lot to be pious. *(Jack bursts ebulliently into the room.)*

JACK. Well! Let me tell you: Everybody is talking about this party. And I mean everybody.

SARA. Oh, yeah?

JACK. Sara, the whole neighborhood is talking. I saw Dr. Cohen on the street.

SARA. Dr. Cohen! Is that so!

JACK. Oh, yeah, I'm telling you: everybody. He was quite grateful for the invitation, Dr. Cohen, wished us all the best.

SARA. Dr. Cohen is coming here?

JACK. Well, no, not exactly. He's a very important man that Dr. Cohen.

SARA. I know!

JACK. You should have seen: He was rushing to the hospital with his little black bag when I saw him. A woman was giving birth, he told me; he couldn't talk, he had to run. I don't envy *his* life, let me tell you. Klein, the tailor, I saw him, too.

SARA. And?

JACK. He said he would try.

SARA. Try?! That doesn't help me. I need to know who's coming. What if there's not enough food?

JACK. There's enough, there's enough! Relax! *I'm* the one who should be nervous. My name is on the line, that's all. Big deal, what's a name? Oh, I even invited a bunch of unfortunate souls off the street, so the *machers'*ll see what a big-hearted *mensch* I am.

SARA. Jack!

JACK. *(Gently corrects her.)* Yankel, Yankel, remember? No more Jack, I'm Yankel again.

SARA. Forgive me: Yankel. It's still so new, I keep forgetting.

JACK. *(To Rivkele, who has been trying to disappear.)* What, you

15

don't say hello to your father anymore? *(To Sara.)* She doesn't say hello? *(Sara nudges Rivkele.)*

RIVKELE. Hello, Papa.

JACK. *(Teasing.)* "Hello, Papa." Come here, I'm not gonna bite you. *(Sees the vestment.)* What's that she's holding?

SARA. *(To Rivkele.)* Show him.

RIVKELE. *(Displays it.)* It's for the vestment, Papa. For the Torah.

JACK. For the — ? Well, how do you like that?! Isn't that wonderful? Where'd it come from?

SARA. Tell him. *(Rivkele says nothing; to Jack.)* She made it.

JACK. *(To Sara.)* No! Yes?

SARA. Yes; she did.

JACK. *(To Rivkele.)* Bring it closer, let me see.

SARA. *(Quietly prodding.)* Go on. *(Rivkele tentatively offers it to Jack. He takes it. He's effusive.)*

JACK. Will you look at this! Isn't that gorgeous?! Such talent! Who knew my little Rivkele had not only beauty but talent? *(To Sara.)* Did *you?*

SARA. Not me.

JACK. It looks professional. Doesn't it?

SARA. *(Nods, while exchanging looks with Rivkele.)* Yes; it does.

JACK. *(To Rivkele.)* You did this all by yourself?

SARA. With her own two hands.

JACK. Where'd she learn how to make a beautiful thing like this?!

SARA. *(Shrugs.)* Here and there.

JACK. *(To Sara.)* You see that? You think you know your own child and then she does something like this? Come, darling, let me give you a kiss. *(Rivkele is reluctant.)* What, you won't let your father kiss you?

SARA. Your father wants to kiss you. Go. *(A beat. Rivkele tentatively goes to him. He pats his lap. Uncomfortably, Rivkele sits on his lap. He kisses her cheek.)*

JACK. Well, now! Was that so terrible?

SARA. *(Shrugs, then.)* I've got to check on that goose.

RIVKELE. *(Suddenly.)* No, Mama! *(She doesn't want to be left alone.)*

SARA. What? It's shpritzing fat all over everything. *(To Yankel.)* You had to have goose … *(Sara goes to the kitchen. He bounces*

Rivkele on his knee while humming a Yiddish song. She gets up.)
JACK. What's the matter? You used to love sitting on my lap.
RIVKELE. I'm too big to sit on your lap.
JACK. Don't be ridiculous. You're still my little girl. Remember we used to ride to Coney Island on Sundays in the summertime, just the two of us, you on my lap? Trolley after trolley, all the way to the end of the line, till we could smell the ocean? And I'd buy you salt water taffy and you'd laugh and chase the waves in your little bathing costume?
RIVKELE. That was a long time ago, Papa.
JACK. How long ago could it be? You're still a child. It seems like yesterday. *(A beat.)* Something happened. What happened?
RIVKELE. Things changed.
JACK. What changed?
RIVKELE. I grew up.
JACK. No no. Why did we stop going? You lost interest in taffy and the long trolley ride, what?
RIVKELE. Papa, may I go to my room now?
JACK. *(Incensed.)* No! When I *tell* you to go to your room, then you may go! *(She is silent; he is remorseful.)* Rivkele ... Come back. I don't mean to yell. You know how much your papa loves you, don't you?
RIVKELE. *(With a sigh.)* Yes, Papa.
JACK. To the ends of the earth, that's how far I would go.
RIVKELE. I know, Papa. I know.
JACK. All I want ... I want you should marry well and have children. I want you should walk down the street with dignity! So when people see you — the so-called respectable people — they look you in the eye — not down at your feet. *(He takes her hand.)* Sweetheart, God is being invited back into this house. You'll see. Things are gonna be different. I promise. *I'm* gonna be different. Once I get that Torah for you ... A holy man, a scribe, wrote one by hand, in beautiful script, for a man who died. He's coming here, this scribe; Reb Eli is bringing him. And I'm offering him a helluva lotta money for it, too, believe me. But, hey, I don't care about that; that's not important. What *is* important is you. *Your* welfare. *Your* future. *(Beaming.)* Eli's been playing matchmaker. He's got his eye on someone for you. A scholar. *(Uncomfortable, she moves away.)* What's

17

wrong? *(She shakes her head, evades him. Sara returns from the kitchen. To Sara.)* I'm embarrassing her. Marriage talk has made her bashful.

SARA. Marriage is God's will. What's to be bashful about? God knows everybody does it.

JACK. *(To Rivkele.)* See? What would you like?

RIVKELE. What do you mean?

JACK. I want to buy you something, a little present. *(Takes out his billfold.)* What should it be? *(She doesn't answer.)* Hm?

SARA. *(To Rivkele.)* Cat got your tongue? Your father wants to buy you something. *(Sotto.)* Take him up on his offer.

JACK. Let's see ... Should it be a doll? A little rag doll? Huh? What.

SARA. She'd like a silk dress and a pair of pretty shoes.

JACK. A silk dress and a pair of shoes? What's wrong with the dresses she has?

SARA. You asked what she wanted.

JACK. *(To Rivkele.)* Is that what you'd like? *(She nods.)* Then why didn't you say so? Here, go buy yourself that dress and those shoes. *(He gives her money.)* You don't know how to say thank you?

RIVKELE. Thank you, Papa. May I go to my room now?

JACK. Okay. Now you may go. *(Rivkele starts to exit. Calls:)* You'll come out for the party, though, won't you.

RIVKELE. Yes, Papa. *(She exits into her room.)*

JACK. *(Pause.)* What's with her?

SARA. *(Shrugs.)* It's the age.

JACK. What more can I do for her than I'm already doing?

SARA. Nothing.

JACK. Sometimes I think she doesn't like me.

SARA. Jack.

JACK. *(Corrects her.)* Yankel. It's true, Sara. I feel like she's passing judgment all the time.

SARA. It's the age.

JACK. I feel like everybody has an opinion about me, and it's not very good.

SARA. What, all of a sudden, in the middle of your life, it matters to you what people think?, what God thinks?

JACK. Of course it matters. What, it shouldn't?

SARA. Public opinion never stopped you before.

JACK. I was never in the middle of my life before. I'm gonna be

18

dead one day, you know.

SARA. God forbid.

JACK. No, honestly. I ask myself, Do I give a damn what people will have to say about me when I'm dead? And the answer comes back, Yeah, I do, I do care. It's not too late to change.

SARA. Well, don't expect miracles. That's all I'm saying. God doesn't hand out miracles like the pickle man from his pushcart. *(Feeling affectionate, he comes up behind her.)*

JACK. You're funny.

SARA. Ha ha. *(He nuzzles his face in her neck.)* What are you doing?

JACK. Can't I have a nibble?

SARA. Nibble. *(Pause. He kisses her neck while she gazes into space.)* When I think of the life I would've had if I'd never met you …

JACK. *(A beat; his ardor cooled.)* You would have died on the street. *(A beat.)* I'm gonna change my clothes. *(He exits. Sara finishes what she's doing and goes to the kitchen. During the above, Rivkele, in bed embroidering, hits a snag, struggles with it, then decides to find Manke. The vestment in hand, Rivkele climbs out of her window, down the fire escape, and stealthily enters the brothel.)*

RIVKELE. *(Whispers.)* Manke? *(A moan draws her to Manke's cubicle, from which we hear creaking bedsprings. Rivkele's impulse is to go but she stops herself and stays to eavesdrop, becoming excited by what she hears. Meanwhile, on the street: Shloyme, a flashily-dressed, streetwise felon, appears, a ribbon-wrapped bundle tucked under his arm. A homeless man approaches from the opposite direction. They converge at the stoop.)*

HOMELESS MAN. This Jack Chapman's place?

SHLOYME. Yeah, what can I do for you?

HOMELESS MAN. He said I should come. I'm a little on the early side.

SHLOYME. You're never too early around here. There's always some girl.

HOMELESS MAN. Girl?

SHLOYME. Yeah. You're here for the girls, right?

HOMELESS MAN. *(Realizing the misunderstanding.)* Oh, no, not the girls, the goose.

SHLOYME. The goose?

HOMELESS MAN. Yeah, he said he's having a party.

SHLOYME. A party, huh? What kind of party?

HOMELESS MAN. I don't know, some kind of party for his daughter.

SHLOYME. For his daughter?

HOMELESS MAN. Look, all I know is he said something about a Torah scroll and a goose.

SHLOYME. A Torah scroll? We talking about the same Jack Chapman?

HOMELESS MAN. Is this his place or not?

SHLOYME. Yeah, this is it. Be my guest, go right on up.

HOMELESS MAN. Thanks. So long.

SHLOYME. *(Calls as he goes.)* And save me a piece of that bird. *(The homeless man goes upstairs. Both Sara and Jack are offstage. The man admires the spread and begins to put food in his pockets. Meanwhile, Shloyme enters the downstairs apartment and is surprised and amused to see Rivkele listening at Manke's cubicle.)* Well, well, well … *(Rivkele gasps. He approaches.)* If it ain't little Goldilocks. What you doing down here, Goldilocks? Picking up a few pointers? *(Mimics panting; cracks himself up.)*

RIVKELE. *(Embarrassed.)* I'm sorry … *(She tries to go past; he blocks her.)*

SHLOYME. Where you going? Look at you: You filled out awfully nice …

RIVKELE. Please …

SHLOYME. Don't go on my account. Sit. Stay and chat awhile. *(He takes her hand, sits her down beside him on the sofa.)*

RIVKELE. Please, I have to go back up. I didn't mean to …

SHLOYME. *(He takes out a Baby Ruth, unwraps it suggestively.)* Want a bite? *(She shakes her head.)* Don't you like chocolate? Sure, you do. Everybody does.

RIVKELE. No, thank you.

SHLOYME. Oh, well. More for me. *(Takes a big bite.)* Mmm … Is that good!

RIVKELE. Please let me go. If my father finds out …

SHLOYME. Hey, I hear he's throwing some kind of party for you, is that right? *(She nods.)* What's this about a Torah scroll? Old Uncle Jack a Yeshiva *bucha* all of a sudden?

RIVKELE. Please, Shloyme.

SHLOYME. Uh! You know my name!

RIVKELE. Didn't my father tell you never to show your face around here again?

SHLOYME. Hey, you know everything, don't you?

RIVKELE. Papa said you took him for a ride.

SHLOYME. *(Amused.)* Something like that.

RIVKELE. I won't say anything if you won't.

SHLOYME. *(Charmed.)* Listen to you! Hey, you're a live one, ain't you, Goldilocks. Come on. Have a little candy. Go ahead. It's not gonna kill ya. *(She hesitates, then slowly takes a bite, her eyes on him.)* Thatta girl. That wasn't too bad, now was it? Pretty tasty, huh?

RIVKELE. Uh-huh.

SHLOYME. See? I wouldn't lie to you. How's Hindl doing?

RIVKELE. Hindl? I don't know.

SHLOYME. She still work down here?

RIVKELE. Uh-huh. As far as I know.

SHLOYME. She ever talk about me?

RIVKELE. How am I supposed to know? Now, please, can I go? If my father … *(He pushes her to her feet.)*

SHLOYME. Go. Get outta here. Get your *toochis* back upstairs. Go! Shoo! *(She heads back up the fire escape, hastily leaving the vestment behind. He finds it.)* What the hell is this? *(He covers his face with it and stretches out to take a nap. Upstairs, Rivkele rushes from her room into the living room, surprising the homeless man, who is busily pocketing food. Other guests come down the street and up the stairs. Jack, now dressed for the occasion, enters.)*

JACK. Well! *(Calls.)* Sara?! Our company is here! *(To the guests.)* Welcome, everyone, welcome!

HOMELESS MAN. *(Bows obsequiously, covering his theft.)* Mr. Chapman, sir!

JACK. Now, now, none of that. You embarrass me. The name's Tshaptshovitsh, actually; I was Chapman for a while but now I'm using Tshaptshovitsh again, the name I was born with. *(Calls.)* Sara, come greet our guests! *(Sara, donning an apron, enters, tries to hide her disdain for the "guests.")*

SARA. Hello.

HOMELESS MAN. Mrs. Chap — *(Looks to Jack.)*

JACK. Tshaptshovitsh. Tshaptshovitsh. And this is our little

Rivkele, the light of our lives. *(He puts his arm around her shoulder; Rivkele averts her eyes.)*

HOMELESS MAN. Oh yes! Quite a looker! *(During the following, more poor people come down the street and arrive upstairs. They're a rowdy bunch. Ad lib party talk.)*

POOR MAN. Our generous host! Our lovely hostess! *(Tries to kiss Sara's hand; Sara recoils.)*

POOR WOMAN #1. *Mazel tov.* May the Torah bring you prosperity and happiness. *(Others concur.)*

JACK. Thank you, thank you. But let's not jump the gun; it isn't mine, not yet. Let's hope and pray. Please, friends, enjoy, help yourselves! *(To Sara.)* See? See? And you were worried there'd be no guests.

SARA. You call these "guests"? Where are all the well-to-do neighbors you were talking about?

JACK. They'll be here. *(To Rivkele.)* Mingle. Schmooze. These people have come to see you.

RIVKELE. No they haven't …

JACK. Go on, sweetheart. Go say hello.

RIVKELE. Must I?

JACK. Yes!

SARA. Do as your father says. Go on.

RIVKELE. *(Uncomfortably, to Poor Man.)* Hello, I'm Rivkele. Welcome to our home.

POOR MAN. *(Belches, then.)* How do you do?

JACK. *(To the guests.)* How about a little entertainment? Yes? Would you like that? *(The guests respond; to Rivkele.)* Sing something.

RIVKELE. What?

JACK. Sing for our guests. Go on.

RIVKELE. What am I supposed to sing?

JACK. Anything.

RIVKELE. I can't …

JACK. Of course you can. A little song is gonna kill you? Sing, darling. *(Announcing.)* My Rivkele will sing for you!

POOR PEOPLE. Wonderful! *(Applause, etc.)*

RIVKELE. No, Papa, please …

JACK. Go on! What's the big deal? They'll hear your sweet little voice.

RIVKELE. I don't want to, Papa, please don't make me sing for these people …

JACK. *(Angered, sotto.)* Enough of this nonsense! You will do as I say. Now sing! *(The gathering eggs her on with applause and words of encouragement. She seems utterly miserable as Jack positions her in the middle of the room. He shushes the assembly and gestures to Rivkele to begin.)*

RIVKELE. *(Sotto; desperately.)* Mama, I can't think of anything to sing! *(Sara, on the sidelines, begins to sing a Yiddish lullaby, gently cuing her daughter. Rivkele sings along, shakily but sweetly. Sara stops singing; Rivkele sings alone. The Orthodox man emerges from Manke's cubicle and exits as Hindl, a weary hooker in her thirties, enters on sore feet. Not realizing Shloyme is asleep on the chaise, she takes off her shoes, rubs her feet. Upstairs, Rivkele finishes her song and the party applauds her. Jack makes a show of his appreciation. The guests resume eating. We focus on the poor women stuffing their faces. Sara winds through with a tray of food and eavesdrops.)*

POOR WOMAN #1. What a shame! She's a lovely girl.

POOR WOMAN #2. I know. You'd think she was raised in a synagogue, not in a place like this.

POOR WOMAN #1. How dreck like those two wound up with such a gem …

POOR WOMAN #2. God only knows.

JACK. *(Approaches, like a host.)* So, how's everything?

POOR WOMAN #2. *(Without missing a beat.)* Ah! We were just saying, what wonderful hosts you are!

JACK. Thank you!

POOR WOMAN #1. And that daughter of yours!

JACK. Isn't she something?

POOR WOMAN #1. Uh!

POOR WOMAN #2. A finer girl you rarely see! You rarely *see* such a girl!

POOR WOMAN #1. Even rabbis don't have such daughters.

JACK. *(Confidentially.)* You wanna know the truth? I agree with you! *(They share a laugh. He hands them more food.)* Here, take, don't be shy, eat, eat, take some more. We wouldn't want you to go home hungry.

POOR PEOPLE. Oh, thank you! Mmm! This is some party! *(Etc.)*

SARA. *(Under her breath, to Rivkele.)* This is who he shows off to? *(Jack taps a glass to get the attention of the gathering.)*

JACK. Ladies and gentlemen. May I have everybody's attention, please. *(They quiet down.)* Up until today, I thought we were all alone. Outcasts. Shunned by our neighbors. But now I look around and see all you wonderful friends and neighbors sharing in our *nakhess* and it makes my heart burst in happiness! I am overwhelmed. Thank you for coming, my friends. Thank you! And enjoy! *L'khaim!*

POOR PEOPLE. L'khaim! *(Amid scattered applause, Sara sidles up to Jack and coaxes him to the stairs.)*

SARA. What is the matter with you?

JACK. Why?

SARA. You talk to these people as if they care about you. They don't care about you. They take your bread and wine and spit at you behind your back! Remember: A *goy* may be *treyf* but his cash is always kosher.

JACK. I'm trying to be a gracious host. I want these people to leave here and tell their friends they were guests of Yankel Tshaptshovitsch and he was a gracious host.

SARA. These people? What do you care what these people think? If we're in the street, they're in the gutter. *(She moves away with a tray of dishes. He lingers on the stairs thinking about what she's said, looks at his watch, seems worried. We fade out and focus on downstairs: Shloyme, still unseen by Hindl, sits up and watches her looking at herself in the mirror.)*

SHLOYME. *(Imitating Jack.)* Why aren't you out on the street?!

HINDL. *(Startled.)* Shloyme! *(He laughs.)* You almost gave me a heart attack. What the hell you doing here?

SHLOYME. Ain't you glad to see me?

HINDL. You want the truth?

SHLOYME. Is that any way to talk?

HINDL. I thought you left the neighborhood. Went to Washington Heights or someplace.

SHLOYME. Yeah, but now I'm back.

HINDL. You're just like the clap, you know that? Just when you think you've gotten rid of it …

SHLOYME. *(Amused.)* Hey. Hindleh. Is that how you talk to the

24

man of your dreams? *(He presents her with the gift. She considers it for a moment before rejecting it.)*

HINDL. Dreams? I don't know about dreams ... Nightmares is more like it. *(She sits and rubs her feet.)* Uy, my feet are killing me. *(He takes over massaging her feet, which she finds suspect.)* What's this for?

SHLOYME. *(Shrugs.)* Can't I rub my girl's feet? I missed you.

HINDL. Yeah, sure. You never did this when we were together.

SHLOYME. I never missed you before.

HINDL. *(Slaps his hand away.)* Two months! Two goddamn months! Not a card, not a word, nothing!

SHLOYME. I'm sorry! Uncle Jack was making life miserable for me downtown. Only the fellas uptown weren't too crazy about me, either.

HINDL. You never should've sold him that booze. Schmuck.

SHLOYME. I didn't know it was bad. How was I supposed to know?

HINDL. You should've known. What kind of way is that to do business?

SHLOYME. What do you want from me? These things happen in business. First you're mad at me for leaving, now you're mad at me for coming back? Hey ... *(He kisses her. She responds, then slaps his face.)* Ow! *(Laughter from upstairs.)*

HINDL. What the hell's going on up there?

SHLOYME. Uncle Jack's having a party. For that precious little girl of his. Boy, I got a good look at her: She's turned into some nice-looking piece. *(Refers to the vestment.)* She left her knitting.

HINDL. That ain't knitting; it's embroidery. He's calling himself Yankel now.

SHLOYME. What do you mean?

HINDL. Says he doesn't want to be called Jack Chapman any-more; that was his Yankee name. Now he's Yankel Tshaptshovitsh.

SHLOYME. What, he's getting religious, "Reb Yankel"? *(They laugh. Pause. He gives her the bundle again. She sits and opens it. It's a pretty shawl. She revels in it for a moment, then stops herself.)*

HINDL. What do you want?

SHLOYME. Why do you always think I want something?

HINDL. Why do you think?

SHLOYME. I came to tell you something.

HINDL. Yeah? Well…? What do you want to tell me?

SHLOYME. *(A beat.)* I found a place.

HINDL. What kind of place?

SHLOYME. An apartment. On Rivington Street. Four rooms. Furnished.

HINDL. Four rooms? What do you need all those rooms for?

SHLOYME. What do you think?

HINDL. *(A beat; catching on.)* Oh …

SHLOYME. I'm gonna open the classiest house on the Lower East Side.

HINDL. Is that so. And how you gonna do that all by yourself?

SHLOYME. I'm not. You're gonna do it with me.

HINDL. So, are you asking me, or what?

SHLOYME. Asking you? I'm telling you.

HINDL. Oh. Excuse me: You're telling me. And you're telling me why?

SHLOYME. So you should know.

HINDL. I see. Well, thanks for telling me.

SHLOYME. Ain't you gonna wish me a *mazel tov*?

HINDL. Oh, sure. *Mazel tov* on your new whorehouse. Use it in good health.

SHLOYME. Thanks. *(Pause. Meanwhile, Jack slips out of the party to the sidewalk to see if other guests are coming.)*

HINDL. You sonofabitch.

SHLOYME. What.

HINDL. You're really not gonna ask me?

SHLOYME. Ask you what?

HINDL. Ask me to marry you.

SHLOYME. Marry you?! Oh, Jack is gonna love that: me stealing one of his girls.

HINDL. He doesn't own me; I'm not their furniture. That Sara looks at me like I'm a, a piece of garbage. So high and mighty she is! Like she never had to walk the streets! I'll be the lady of the house. I'll be real good at it, too. You know I would. I've got a good head for business. I'll run a tight house for you, Shloym, you know I will.

SHLOYME. Easy, will ya? Slow down. There is no house! There's a vacant four-room apartment! Can't have a house without girls.

HINDL. I'll get us girls.

SHLOYME. You? What, you're a white slave trader and you didn't tell me?

HINDL. What if I get you Manke?

SHLOYME. Manke?! You're gonna get me Manke?

HINDL. If I get you Manke ... She brings in a lot of business, you know, more than anybody. If I get her for you ... Marry me. Make an honest woman out of me, Shloym.

SHLOYME. Too late for that.

HINDL. You gotta get me out of here, Shloym. You gotta take me with you.

SHLOYME. Take you where? I'm only talking about Rivington Street!

HINDL. I don't care, I'm dying here, Shloym. *(She leads him to her cubicle. She kisses him. Sultry, suggestive:)* I'll take care of you. You know how well I take care of you, don'tcha? Don't I take good care of my man? Huh? Huh?

SHLOYME. *(Succumbing.)* Aw shit ... *(Shloyme pulls the curtain. Meanwhile, Sara has joined Jack on the street with a plate of food.)*

SARA. You should eat something.

JACK. You were right: No one else is coming. No Reb Eli, no Scribe. We're stuck with the dregs.

SARA. Look: You've got a place to live? Stay there. You've got bread to eat? Eat it. Enjoy. But don't try going where you're not wanted, and don't try being what you're not. Have you forgotten who we are?

JACK. Who are we? Have we robbed anybody? Murdered anybody? I run a business! The need is there, we provide the service. Economics, pure and simple. That's how it works. For this I should be punished? This is America! *(Downstairs, Hindl and Shloyme:)*

HINDL. Whataya say? Huh, Shloym? Huh?

SHLOYME. I'm starving; I wonder what they got to eat up there. *(She grabs him by his collar.)* Hey!

HINDL. I want an answer. If I bring you Manke, will you marry me.

SHLOYME. Knock it off! You're cutting off my circulation!

HINDL. Will you?

SHLOYME. Okay! I'll marry you! I'll marry you! *(She releases him and kisses him all over.)*

HINDL. Thank you thank you thank you!

SHLOYME. *(Overlap.)* Jesus! Now can we get something to eat?

HINDL. Sure, let's go stuff our faces. *(Hindl and Shloyme encounter Jack and Sara on the stairs.)*

SHLOYME. "Reb" Yankel!

JACK. Uh! You!

SHLOYME. Sara, you're looking the respectable woman this evening …

SARA. Drop dead.

SHLOYME. How long you been holy, "Reb Yankel"? Since lunchtime?

JACK. Get out of here. Now! Go!

HINDL. *(Helping herself to food.)* Is that any way to treat your old friends?

SARA. Old friends?! Ha!

JACK. *Goniff*! The nerve of you showing your face around here!

SHLOYME. We came to pay our respects. To little Rivkele.

JACK. Yeah? Well, nobody invited you.

SHLOYME. You invite bums in off the street but business associates you throw out?

JACK. *(Over " … you throw out?")* "Business associates"?! You call what you do business?!

SARA. *(Over " … business?!")* Don't even speak to them. Get them out of here!

HINDL. *(Hefts a fork.)* Is this real silver?

SARA. *(Snatches the fork.)* Out of my house. Vermin!

HINDL. The hell with your house. We're gonna have a house of our own.

SHLOYME. Hindl …

JACK. *(Overlap; skeptical.)* Your own house, is that so?

HINDL. That's right. Shloyme's gonna marry me.

SHLOYME. *(To Hindl.)* You got a big mouth, you know that?

SARA. *(Overlap.)* Marry you?!

HINDL. Why? *That* prize married *you. (To Shloyme.)* Tell them!

SHLOYME. She's gonna be my girl now, what do you think about that?

SARA. Oh, really! I wish you luck!

JACK. *(Overlap; to Shloyme.)* I'm not gonna discuss this with you up here. *(Escorting him.)* Downstairs, the both of you, now!

SHLOYME. *(Pulling away from him.)* Hey! Watch the hands!

JACK. Downstairs! If you have anything to say to me, you say it downstairs. Upstairs, I don't know you and you don't know me.

SHLOYME. I got news for you, Yankel Chapawhozitz or whatever you're calling yourself these days: upstairs, downstairs, the devil's the same all over.

JACK. Out of here! Now!

SARA. *(Taking food from Hindl.)* Don't you have work to do? You barely earn your keep anymore!

HINDL. Oh, yeah? Let's see *you* go downstairs and peddle *your* ass, see how much *you* bring in!

SHLOYME. *(To Hindl.)* Better yet, tell her to send down little Rivkele. *(He and Hindl laugh.)*

JACK. *(Attacking him.)* You sonofabitch! How dare you! How dare you even speak her name! You are scum! Scum! *(A fight ensues. The remaining guests disperse. During the commotion, Manke emerges from her cubicle downstairs and listens. Upstairs, Rivkele stands in her doorway, fascinated. Jack roughhouses Shloyme down the stairs to the sidewalk and puts a switchblade to his throat.)*

SARA. Oh, my God! Jack!

HINDL. Shloyme!

SARA. *(Over, to Jack.)* Stop it!

JACK. *(To Shloyme.)* If I ever hear you speak her name again …
If I ever see your face again … *(Meanwhile, Eli, a matchmaker and all-around go-between, and Reb Aaron, the Scribe, an ancient, mysterious, pious man, come down the street.)*

ELI. *(Entering; overlap.)* Oh, my oh my! Gentlemen! Gentlemen! What's all this?

SARA. Jack! Reb Eli. *(Jack stops battling Shloyme.)*

JACK. Reb Eli, hello. *(To Shloyme and Hindl, controlling his rage.)* Go.

ELI. Shame on you! You should be rejoicing, not fighting. *(Jack's eyes are on Shloyme and Hindl, who is nursing Shloyme's bloody lip.)*

JACK. Forgive me. I was evicting some riff-raff. They were just leaving.

SHLOYME. *(Fixing his collar.)* Come, Hindleh. I can tell when we're not welcome. So long, "Reb" Yankel. *(To Hindl.)* Get a load of who he's taking up with. Next thing you know, he'll be running for mayor. *(Hindl laughs. They exit brusquely past Eli and the Scribe. Jack leads them upstairs.)*

JACK. Pardon the intrusion. Please: Come upstairs. You open your home to the neighborhood, you're bound to get a few rotten apples. *(A nervous laugh.)*

ELI. Yes. Well. *(To the Scribe, making introductions.)* Aaron ... This is Mr. Chapman.

JACK. Tshaptshovitsh. Remember?

ELI. Yes, yes, excuse me. Tshap — ?

JACK. Tshaptshovitsh.

ELI. Mr. Tshaptshovitsh.

JACK. Hello, sir. Welcome. Welcome to my home. *(Jack extends his hand, which the Scribe pointedly doesn't shake. Jack withdraws his hand in embarrassment.)*

SCRIBE. *(To Eli, his eyes on Jack.)* This is the man who wants to buy the Torah scroll?

ELI. Yes.

SCRIBE. *(Coolly.)* Sholem-aleykhem.

JACK. *Aleykhem-sholem. (Sara bows, steps back respectfully as the Scribe comes forward.)* Please, sir. Sit down. Sara? *(Sara sets out a chair for the Scribe.)* Some schnapps? Hm? *(The Scribe shrugs, nods. Jack fills glasses, with Sara's help, gives them to the men.)*

ELI. L'khaim.

JACK. L'khaim. *(Eli and Jack down their drinks but the Scribe does not, unnerving them. Sara steps forward to brightly offer some food but Jack restrains her.)*

SCRIBE. *(To Eli, while looking at Jack.)* This is the man?

ELI. Yes, Aaron, this is the man. He doesn't have a son, so he wants to serve God by purchasing his own handwritten copy of the Torah. *(To Jack.)* Isn't that right?

JACK. Yes. *(Eli prompts him to be more positive.)* Oh, yes! For my daughter's dowry. I thought if I could buy the one you —

ELI. Just answer yes or no. *(Continuing, to the Scribe.)* This is very honorable, no? We must celebrate this in any man.

SCRIBE. Tell me: What sort of man is he?

ELI. What sort of man?

30

JACK. Well, you see, Rebbe …

ELI. *(Cutting him off.)* What difference does it make? He's a Jew, is he not?

JACK. True. I'm a Jew.

ELI. An ordinary Jew. If you mean, is he a scholar? No. The answer is no.

JACK. No. No scholar.

ELI. But does every Jew have to be a scholar?

JACK. That's right!

ELI. If a Jew wants to do a mitzvah, like this, don't we owe him something? A helping hand at least? Now, come, Aaron, let's drink … *(Refills his and Jack's glasses.)* L'khaim.

JACK. *L'khaim. (Eli and Jack drink; once more, the Scribe does not.)*

SCRIBE. Does he know how to conduct himself with a holy book?

ELI. Of course he knows.

JACK. Of course I know.

ELI. What Jew doesn't know what a Torah is?

JACK. Exactly. I was bar mitzvah forty-odd years ago, in Warsaw. A Jew is what I am.

ELI. *(Prepares another round.)* L'khaim, l'khaim … Let us toast. May God grant us better times.

JACK. Better times. *L'khaim. (Jack drinks with Eli. The Scribe does not.)*

SCRIBE. A Torah is a magnificent thing.

JACK. Oh, I know.

SCRIBE. Remember that.

JACK. I do, Rebbe, I do.

ELI. Shh. Listen.

SCRIBE. One handwritten scroll enfolds the entire world. Each Torah is like the very Tablets of the Law that were handed down to Moses from Mount Sinai. Every line, every stroke of the pen, is written in purity and holiness. And where a home has a scroll of the Torah, then God is there, too. So, for that reason alone, it must be kept free of contamination. Do you understand what that means?

JACK. *(Terrified by the Scribe's speech.)* Yes, Rebbe.

SCRIBE. Do you understand that responsibility?

31

JACK. Yes, Rebbe, listen, I must tell you something …

ELI. *(To Yankel.)* What are you doing?

JACK. I must tell him everything. I must tell him the truth.

ELI. *(Quietly, to Jack, trying to save the deal.)* No no no …

JACK. Rebbe, I am a sinful man …

ELI. *(Overlap.)* Sh sh sh. *(To Scribe.)* Rebbe, the man is a penitent, see?, so we have to help him, right? The Talmud says so. Doesn't it?

JACK. I got caught up in business. I forgot about God.

ELI. *(Sotto, to Jack.)* Quiet!

JACK. I changed my name. I denied who I was. I tried to hide from God.

ELI. Let me handle this, will you!

JACK. I'm tired of hiding, Rebbe, I don't want to hide anymore.

ELI. What it comes down to is …

JACK. I've taken back my name. My Jewish name, the name I was born with.

ELI. What it comes down to is respect. As long as you respect the Torah, and watch your tongue, and be pious and modest, what could go wrong?

SCRIBE. A single word, heaven help us!, one single word could disgrace the Torah, and then a huge calamity might descend on not just you but on all Jews, everywhere!

JACK. *(Agitated.)* Rebbe … Listen … I'm not worthy of your presence here, under my roof.

ELI. Don't…!

JACK. I have to say this. Rebbe, I am a sinful man.

ELI. *(To himself.)* Uy.

JACK. *(Holding Sara by her shoulders.)* She is a sinful woman.

SARA. Yankel.

JACK. We don't have the right to even touch a Torah scroll. But there … *(Points to Rivkele's room.)* In there, Rebbe … An angel lives there … Let me show you. *(He goes into Rivkele's room, surprising her, takes her by the hand and leads her into the living room.)* This is my Rivkele. The scroll is for her, Rebbe, not for me. *(Takes her hands, lovingly examines them.)* These hands, Rebbe, look at these hands. These are the purest hands imaginable. *(To Rivkele.)* Go, darling, show the rebbe what you're making for the Torah.

RIVKELE. *(Panicked but trying not to show it.)* What?

JACK. The vestment. Show him.

RIVKELE. Um …

JACK. Show him.

RIVKELE. Oh, Papa, must I?

JACK. Yes.

RIVKELE. But … It's … it's not finished.

JACK. So what? Go get it.

RIVKELE. *(Tearfully.)* Please, Papa … don't make me … Please don't …

SARA. *(Urges gently.)* Yankel …

JACK. *(To Rivkele.)* Uh, okay, dearest. *(To the men.)* She's shy. You see what humility? *(He takes her hands and displays them for the Scribe.)* These hands, Rebbe, have embroidered the finest vestment for a Torah I have ever seen. Wait till you see. You will be amazed. My hands won't touch your Torah scroll. *(Points to Sara.)* Her hands won't, either. But these, *(Rivkele's.)* these hands will. She'll take care of it. And honor it. It will stay in her room. And when she marries, she can take it with her wherever she and her husband may go.

ELI. *(To the Scribe.)* Isn't that wonderful?

JACK. "Forget your father," I'll tell her. "Forget your mother. Have pure, decent children of your own." *(Quietly, to Rivkele.)* Now, go, sweetheart. Go to your room. *(Kisses her head; smiles, watches as she goes.)* Rebbe, we are the sinful people. *(Meaning Sara and himself.)*

SARA. *(Under her breath.)* All right, already, Yankel.

JACK. Not her. This is why I went over to the synagogue and went up to this man, *(Meaning Eli.)* this man who is so wise about other peoples' lives, and I said to him, "Reb Eli, I need your help. I am a sinful man, but how can I protect my daughter from sin? I may be doomed but how can I save her? How can I make sure she gets the kind of decent husband she deserves?" And he said to me, "Buy a Torah, put it in your house." He told me you had just copied one, for a man who died. Rebbe, that's all I want, that's all I ask. Please, sir. I must have that scroll. *(Eli confers with the Scribe. Jack and Sara watch expectantly as the old man weighs his verdict.)*

SCRIBE. We will need a minyan.

ELI. *(Relieved.)* No problem. We'll go to the synagogue, we'll find ten men.

JACK. *(Overlap.)* Thank you, thank you.

ELI. *(Refills glasses.)* Now, good: Let's drink. *L'khaim.*

JACK. *L'khaim.*

SCRIBE. *L'khaim.*

ELI. You see, Reb Aaron? Even if a Jew sins, he's still a Jew. A Jewish soul wants the best for his child. *(To Jack.)* God loves a penitent, true. But you have to make donations to the scholars.

JACK. Of course.

ELI. If you're not a scholar yourself, then you have to support scholarship. Because *al toyrah oylem oymeyd:* On the Torah rests the whole world. Isn't that right, Reb Aaron? Isn't that the way it is? *(The Scribe nods; to Jack.)* Give up your old ways and support scholars.

JACK. Oh, I will, I will.

ELI. Forget the path you've been on, and follow a different path.

JACK. I am, I will.

ELI. Do these things and eventually God will forgive you.

JACK. I'm gonna follow a different path, the path that leads to God. *(Eli puts his arm around Jack, walks him away from the Scribe.)*

ELI. I've made some progress in lining up that bridegroom for your daughter.

JACK. Oh, yes?

ELI. A scholar. Who's going to college!

JACK. You hear this, Sara? College!

ELI. And now that you have a Torah for a dowry?!

JACK. Oh, thank God!

ELI. Come, let's find a minyan and rejoice in the Holy Book.

JACK. Wait. You're saying I can walk down the street with men such as yourselves?

ELI. Why not?

JACK. *(Moved.)* You're not ashamed to be seen with me?

ELI. Look, if God forgives you, then we can certainly forgive you. Isn't that so, Reb Aaron?

SCRIBE. *(Shrugs.)* Who can say? Our God is a God of mercy, a God of compassion — but we mustn't forget: He is also a God of vengeance. *(Looks at the fading light.)* Hm, it's getting late. Come, if we're going to synagogue, we must go now ... *(The Scribe exits the apartment, starts going down the stairs.)*

JACK. What did he mean by that?

ELI. Don't worry about it. *(To Sara.)* You think maybe you can prepare a little something for when we come back?

SARA. Consider it done.

JACK. Reb Eli, I am so grateful. How can I ever repay you?

ELI. Let me tell you about our new scholarship fund.

JACK. Could it be in my name?

ELI. Of course it can. If the donation is sizable enough ... *(They go down the stairs and down the street. Sara primps in front of a mirror and putters as she calls to Rivkele, who is lying dreamily in bed, alone in her room.)*

SARA. Rivkele!

RIVKELE. Yes, Mama?

SARA. The men have gone to get a minyan. They'll be back any minute. Put on your nice blue dress. Hurry.

RIVKELE. Yes, Mama. *(She gets out of bed. Meanwhile, Manke climbs the ladder of the fire escape and soon appears at Rivkele's window. Rivkele is terribly excited to see her but dares not exclaim; Manke slowly moves toward Rivkele as Sara continues speaking from the next room. The girls hardly take their eyes off each other.)*

MANKE. *(Whispers.)* Are you all right? *(Rivkele nods.)* I had to see you.

SARA. I can't believe this day has come.

RIVKELE. *(Whispers, to Manke.)* You'd better go. My mother ...

MANKE. *(Touches Rivkele's lips to silence her.)* Shhh ...

SARA. Your father has talked about this day for so long. Reb Eli says it's looking very good for this bridegroom! *Kunna horre*, I should keep my mouth shut. Do you need help in there?

RIVKELE. No! I don't need help. *(Her eyes on Manke.)* Tell me about my bridegroom, Mama. *(Manke helps her out of her party dress.)*

SARA. No, no, we mustn't talk about him. It's bad luck.

RIVKELE. Please, Mama, tell me about him. I want to know. What is he like?

SARA. Well ... he's very special.

RIVKELE. Yes?

SARA. Oh, yes. A treasure.

RIVKELE. A treasure?! Yes!

SARA. A scholar. Very smart. And kind.

RIVKELE. Yes. So kind.

SARA. An honest man. A good provider.

RIVKELE. Where will we go?

SARA. He'll take you to live in a fine house. Filled with light. With trees all around. And your children — respectable, decent children — will run through the fields, laughing.

RIVKELE. What does he look like? Is he handsome, Mama? *(Manke takes Rivkele's face in her hands and kisses her passionately on the lips. They caress one another.)*

SARA. Oh, yes! Very handsome. Beautiful, really.

RIVKELE. Yes. So so beautiful.

SARA. Clear, pale skin — white almost.

RIVKELE. Yes.

SARA. Shiny black hair. And a smile…! Such a smile!

RIVKELE. What about his eyes, Mama. Tell me about my bridegroom's eyes.

SARA. His eyes are dark. But they sparkle. Like jewels.

RIVKELE. Yes! They do! And his hands, are his hands gentle?

SARA. Yes. And strong.

RIVKELE. *(Responds to Manke's touch.)* Mmm. Will he touch me and caress my hair?

SARA. Yes, always.

RIVKELE. Will he love me, Mama?

SARA. Will he love you?

RIVKELE. Yes. Will he love me, my bridegroom? Will he?

SARA. Yes, of course he will. He'll love you completely, with all his heart. *(We hear sung prayers as holy men in black — ten in all, the minyan, including Jack, Eli, and the Scribe, who holds the Torah aloft, seemingly glowing from within — come down the street and begin to go upstairs.)* Oh, my God! They're coming! He's back with the men! Hurry hurry hurry! They're on their way! *(Manke and Rivkele share a parting kiss. Rivkele gets into her dress as Manke descends the fire escape ladder. The men file into the upstairs apartment. Fade out.)*

ACT TWO

A light spring rain. Later that night. Lights up on the gleaming Torah, now hanging in a cabinet on the wall in Rivkele's room. She is in her nightclothes, dreamily humming while brushing her hair. During the following, she gets ready for bed, turns out her light. Her haunting song continues while Manke comes down the street with a customer walking a few steps behind her. Both are holding umbrellas. She enters the downstairs apartment first; the man follows. He gives her money. They go into her cubicle. Shloyme and Hindl come down the street arguing.

HINDL. He said hello! What do you want me to do, ignore him? He's just being friendly.

SHLOYME. Friendly?! That ain't "friendly," that's giving you the eye.

HINDL. You're crazy! I know him from the neighborhood. I walk past his hardware store a dozen times a day.

SHLOYME. I saw the way he looked at you, I saw that look.

HINDL. What look?

SHLOYME. "Well hello there, Hindl."

HINDL. That's just Moish. That's how he talks. He's a character.

SHLOYME. Did you do it with him?

HINDL. Oh God, Shloym, what is the matter with you?

SHLOYME. *Did* you?

HINDL. What, all of a sudden you're jealous?

SHLOYME. Answer me: Did you screw him.

HINDL. You're nuts, you know that? *(He grabs her by her arm.)*

SHLOYME. Did you?! Did you?! You did, didn't you!

HINDL. Let go of me!

SHLOYME. Did he pay? Huh? Did he, you stinking filthy whore? Did he?

37

HINDL. No! *(Shloyme tosses her aside; she yelps.)*

SHLOYME. And I said I would marry you?! What was I thinking?! What the hell was I thinking?!

HINDL. *(Over "What the hell ... ")* He was nice to me! Don't I deserve someone nice now and then?

SHLOYME. *(Over " ... now and then?")* I said I'd go into *business* with you?!

HINDL. You'd gone away! How was I supposed to know you were coming back? I thought I was never gonna see you again!

SHLOYME. *(Over "I thought ... ")* I must be outta my mind! We'll go broke! You give it away!

HINDL. *(Over " ... outta my mind!")* You're my man, not him. I don't give a damn about him! He says hello, I'll cross the street —

SHLOYME. You're secondhand goods!

HINDL. Please, Shloym, let's not fight. Come on, baby, don't ... *(She tries to kiss him; he pushes her away.)*

SHLOYME. Get offa me!

HINDL. I promised you Manke. Remember? You said if I got you Manke ...

SHLOYME. Get *offa* me, I said! *(He tosses her aside and storms down the street.)*

HINDL. Shloyme, no! *(She sobs; her face streaks with mascara. Basha and Reyzl run laughing down the street from the opposite direction, their clothing drenched by the downpour.)*

REYZL. Ooo, I love the rain, don't you?

BASHA. Rain makes me think of the orchard back home ... Rain falling on the leaves ... My mama, may she rest in peace, her borscht on the stove ... *(Inhales.)* I can smell it.

REYZL. I remember the goats we had, grazing in the rain. I can smell them, too! *(They laugh.)*

BASHA. Oh, and all my old friends, my girlfriends, oh, God, I miss them. They'd be out dancing in the fields in a rain like this. And I'd be dancing with them, barefoot and drenched, far from the *shtetl,* far from our fathers.

REYZL. Would he get mad, your father?

BASHA. Oh, God, would he!

REYZL. Mine used to come after me with a branch! Caught me with a boy once, hit me so hard, it left a scar. See? *(Shows her arm.)*

BASHA. *(Winces.)* Oooh. *My* father was a butcher. He had all these sharp knives. He didn't like something I did? He'd put a knife to my throat and threaten to stick it in!

REYZL. Oh, God!

BASHA. I don't know if he's alive or dead and I don't care.

REYZL. Basha!

BASHA. He wanted me to marry Notke, the other butcher in town. It was all arranged.

REYZL. What was he like?

BASHA. Notke? Uch, he was awful. These big hairy hands, and he always smelled like beef! *(Reyzl laughs.)* He did! He was disgusting. The thought of spending the rest of my life with him, those rough hairy hands touching me, stinking of blood ...

REYZL. Ich ... So what happened? *(They enter the brothel. Hindl, still unseen, shields her tear-streaked face.)*

BASHA. I ran away. To America. My mama didn't want me to be a butcher's wife like she was. She gave me every last *scheckl* she saved to pay my way.

REYZL. Ohhh ...

BASHA. The last time I saw her, my boat was pulling away. She ran all the way to the end of the dock, till there was nowhere left to run ... *(A faraway voice.)* "Goodbye, Basheleh! Find a better life! God be with you!" *(Silence. Saddened:)* Some "better life." *(Reyzl puts her arm around her.)* Thank God she didn't live to find out what I do.

HINDL. And what's wrong with what we do?

REYZL. *(Surprised to see her.)* Hindl.

HINDL. Are we any different from the shopgirls? Or the factory girls, or the secretaries? We're all out to earn a buck. We all gotta survive. You think the middle-class wives are any better off? They gotta work hard for their keep, too — by making their fat husbands happy.

REYZL. Hey. What's with your face?

HINDL. Nothing.

REYZL. You been crying?

HINDL. No ... *(Fixing her face in the mirror.)* Just the rain.

BASHA. *(Still haunted by her mother.)* She comes to me sometimes.

HINDL. Who?

BASHA. My poor dead *mamaleh*, from deep in her grave.

REYZL. You see her?! *(Basha nods.)* When?

BASHA. At night.

HINDL. What are you talking about?

BASHA. She comes to me, her shroud all torn and covered in mud ...

REYZL. Uch! What does she do?

BASHA. She gets into bed with me. *(Reyzl gasps.)* She rips hair from my head and scratches my face with her nails.

REYZL. Why?

BASHA. Because of my sins, the terrible things I've done.

HINDL. *(Spooked.)* Stop it. I don't like this; I don't like it one bit.

REYZL. *(Over "... one bit.")* Does she speak?

BASHA. She doesn't speak, she cries. She howls in shame ... *(A haunted, faraway voice.)* "Basha, how could you!? This is not what I wanted for you!"

HINDL. All right, already! Enough about sins! Enough about ghosts! You're giving me the creeps! *(Meanwhile, Jack, holding a basket of food, comes downstairs.)*

JACK. Hell-o-o!

REYZL. *(Quietly.)* Oh, no!

HINDL. *(To the girls.)* What does he want?

JACK. *(Enters cheerfully.)* Well! Good evening, girls.

BASHA. Evening.

JACK. Some night, hm? Any business at all? *(Basha and Reyzl shake their heads.)*

HINDL. Manke. She's got someone.

JACK. Leave it to Manke. So ... How are my girls?

REYZL. Don't worry, we're going back out.

BASHA. We just came in to change; we got soaked.

JACK. That's all right, I'm not complaining. You hear me complaining? I didn't come here to yell.

REYZL. No?

JACK. No! I came to tell you girls to call it a night.

BASHA. *(Incredulous.)* You did?

JACK. Stay in! Keep dry! God forbid you should get a cold.

REYZL. You mean you're not gonna make us walk the streets in the rain?

JACK. No no no. Better you should stay in and keep your health.

BASHA. Yeah? But you always said, Don't come back unless it's with a customer.

JACK. That was the *old* Yankel. This is the *new* Yankel.

HINDL. The new Yankel, huh.

JACK. That's right: the one who's changing his ways.

HINDL. You mean Yankel, the *mensch,* not Yankel, the pimp?

JACK. *(With a smile.)* You're not gonna get a rise out of me tonight, Hindl. Not tonight. Tonight I begin again. I'm so happy, I could dance around the room! *(He sings and spins Basha, who is aghast.)*

BASHA. Mister…!

HINDL. What's with you?!

JACK. What's with *me? God* is with me.

HINDL. *Uy vey.*

JACK. Make fun all you want. Look what I brought you … *(He unveils the splendid basket of food. The girls exclaim but hesitate.)*

HINDL. Okay, where's the catch?

JACK. There is no catch. My!, you're so suspicious, Hindl. Does there always have to be a catch?

HINDL. Generally speaking…?

JACK. Can't I give my girls a little treat now and then? Huh? Look at all this beautiful food going to waste! I want you to have it. Take! Help yourselves! *(The girls warily help themselves.)* There you go! Don't be shy.

BASHA and REYZL. Oh, thank you … Thank you, Mister. *(They savor the bread, etc.)*

JACK. Uncle. Call me Uncle. No one can say I'm not a good employer. Look at the benefits. There! Now isn't that good?

BASHA and REYZL. Mmm, yes … Delicious … *(Etc.)*

JACK. Whatever you do, don't tell Sara I gave you. She thinks I'm too generous as it is. *(To Hindl.)* Take. It's only gonna go bad.

HINDL. I don't take charity. Not from the likes of you.

JACK. Oh, I see. Well, aren't you superior. You don't want my food? Fine. *(A beat.)* Your darling boyfriend around? Excuse me: your fiancé.

HINDL. What do you care?

JACK. Give him a *challah.* Tell him it's on me.

HINDL. You gotta be kidding.

JACK. No! I told you: I'm not the same man I was when I woke up this morning. God has been invited back into my house. He's there. He's right upstairs. Big changes are happening around here.

HINDL. Oh, yeah, what kind of changes?

JACK. *Big* changes. As soon as I get my Rivkele married off ... I'm closing up shop.

HINDL. You're what?!

BASHA. *(Overlap.)* What do you mean?

JACK. I'm getting out of the business.

HINDL. What do you mean you're getting out of the business? You're going straight?

JACK. That's right.

HINDL. What are you gonna do?

JACK. Taxi medallions.

HINDL. *Taxi* medallions?

BASHA. *(Overlap.)* Taxis?!

JACK. Mark my words: Taxis are gonna be the next big thing in this town. I'm buying a whole fleet's worth.

HINDL. Unbelievable.

BASHA. And what happens to us?!

REYZL. Are you kicking us out?

JACK. Nobody's kicking you out.

HINDL. Sure.

BASHA. I *live* here; this is my *home!* The only home I've ever had here!

REYZL. *(Over "The only home ... ")* Where are we supposed to go?

JACK. *(Overlap; calming them down.)* Shh shh shh ... Don't get hysterical.

HINDL. *(Overlap.)* What does *he* care? He doesn't give a damn what happens to us.

JACK. Quiet, you! *(To the others.)* You think I'd just throw you out on the street? I'll send you off with a few bucks to get you started. A little something, you'll be fine.

REYZL. And do what? How we gonna live?

BASHA. *(Over "How we gonna ... ")* This is all I've ever done; I don't know how to do anything else!

REYZL. Me, neither!

JACK. You're young, you'll find husbands.

BASHA. *(Tearful.)* Who's gonna want me?

JACK. *(Soothing.)* Basha …

BASHA. *(Continuous.)* What kind of man'll want to marry a girl like me?

HINDL. Shloyme's marrying *me* …

JACK. You see that?

HINDL. We're opening up a house of our own. You can come work for us.

JACK. Uh! You see that?!

BASHA. *(To Hindl.)* Work for *you?* What makes you think I'd want to come work for *you?*

HINDL. Well, the hell with *you!*

REYZL. I'd rather starve to death!

HINDL. The hell with both of you! I offer you a roof over your heads and this is how you talk to me?

BASHA. Screw you!

HINDL. *(Continuous.)* We'll see how you feel when winter comes and you're freezing your asses off!

BASHA. Oh, yeah?

JACK. *(Overlap.)* Girls, girls! Enough of this! Really, now. You should be ashamed of yourselves. There's a Torah upstairs now. Show a little respect. Now go to sleep and get some rest, all of you. Go!

REYZL. Good night, Uncle.

JACK. Good night. And make sure Manke gets some food. *(He starts to go.)*

BASHA. Yes, Uncle. Good night.

HINDL. Hey. Reb Yankel. You forgot something. *(She balls up Rivkele's vestment and throws it at him. He picks it up.)*

JACK. *(Realizes.)* Oh, my God … What is this doing here?!

HINDL. I dunno.

JACK. Did you steal it?

HINDL. No!

JACK. *(To Hindl, grabbing her arm.)* Did you?! Did you snatch it upstairs from the party?

HINDL. *(Overlap.)* No! Let go of me!

JACK. You stole it when no one was looking!

HINDL. I did not! Stop it! You're hurting me!

BASHA. Leave her alone!

JACK. *(To Basha.)* Did *you*? Did you sneak upstairs?

BASHA. No!

JACK. *(Grabs Reyzl.)* Did *you*?!

REYZL. Uncle! Please!

JACK. Then how did it get here? Huh? Magic? Somebody stole it!

HINDL. Nobody stole it, dear, repentant Uncle.

JACK. What?

HINDL. Somebody left it behind.

JACK. What are you talking about, left it behind?

HINDL. Rivkele! Rivkele left it!

JACK. Rivkele?!

HINDL. Yes, Uncle. Your precious Rivkele. She was down here! *(Jack grabs a bottle and threatens to hit her with it. She cowers.)*

JACK. How dare you! How dare you say such a thing!

HINDL. *(Overlap.)* She came down to see Manke!

JACK. What?

HINDL. She and Manke are friends! They're friends! Manke's been teaching her how to embroider! This is Manke's work! She did it.

JACK. That's not true! Rivkele did it! She told me herself!

HINDL. You stupid, blind man! She comes down here! Your darling daughter!

JACK. Liar!

HINDL. I'm not lying! It's the truth!

JACK. *(Continuous.)* I want you out of here first thing in the morning. You hear me? First thing!

HINDL. With pleasure. *(He releases her.)*

JACK. Now, go! All of you! Go to bed! I want you out of my sight! *(Reyzl and Basha scurry off to their beds. Jack runs upstairs with the vestment. Hindl lingers in the shadows. Jack bursts into Rivkele's room. She wakens, frightened.)*

RIVKELE. Papa!

JACK. Look what I found downstairs! Look! Look! *(Sara appears in a robe.)*

SARA. *(Over "Look!")* Jack! What's going on?

JACK. *(To Rivkele.)* What was this doing there? Huh? Huh?

RIVKELE. *(Crying hysterically.)* Papa, please!

44

JACK. *(Continuous; slapping her with the vestment.)* I want an answer! Have you been going downstairs?! Have you? *(Etc.)*

SARA. Jack, leave the girl alone!

RIVKELE. *(Over "Have you...?")* Papa, don't! Please, Papa! *(Etc.)*

SARA. The Torah! What is the matter with you?!

RIVKELE. Mama?

SARA. Shhh ... *(Sara comforts Rivkele, tucks her back into bed. She leads Jack into the other room. Rivkele listens.)*

JACK. That Hindl, you know what she said? She said Rivkele's been down there!

SARA. What?

JACK. *(Continuous.)* Can you imagine? That whore! Such lies! I could kill her!

SARA. I have to tell you something.

JACK. *(Continuous.)* It's jealousy, *that's* what it is. Jealousy!

SARA. Listen to me, Yankel. Quiet. You're not gonna like this.

JACK. Don't tell me that; I hate when you tell me that.

SARA. Sit down.

JACK. I don't want to sit down.

SARA. All right, *don't* sit down.

JACK. What. Tell me.

SARA. *(Sighs.)* This isn't the easiest life we've made for ourselves, you know.

JACK. Yeah, yeah. So?

SARA. All I want is for my family to be happy; I want *you* to be happy, I want *Rivkele* to be happy. Sometimes that means I have to look the other way.

JACK. What are you talking about?

SARA. It's true. Hindl is telling the truth. Manke's been teaching her how to embroider.

JACK. Oh, my God.

SARA. Rivkele wanted to learn, so I mentioned that Manke did nice needlework and ...

JACK. You did?!

SARA. I'm very sorry, what's done is done!

JACK. What have I been talking about all these years?! What have I been saying?!

SARA. *(Over "What have I been saying?")* They're just girls! Like

45

sisters!

JACK. "Sisters"?! What's the matter with you?! Manke is a whore! You want your daughter talking to whores?

SARA. The girl has no friends! She has no friends! Who does she have?

JACK. She has you and me! She has her family!

SARA. She needs more than us. What world are you living in where things are so simple? She's growing up! She's curious about the world! She's lonely! She goes to school and she comes home to her room! Those are the rules you insist she keep. What kind of life is that?

JACK. What do you want, you want your daughter to end up like you?! Huh? Is that what you want?! Like mother like daughter?

SARA. *(A beat; hurt.)* No. God forbid she should end up like me.

JACK. There's already one whore in the family, what's another one? Why not?, it's the family business!

SARA. You made me a whore.

JACK. I "made" you...?

SARA. I was practically a child. No older than Rivkele.

JACK. How did I "make" you? With promises of food in your stomach, clothes on your back? Your teeth were falling out when I found you; you were skin and bones. "Saved" you is more like it.

SARA. *(Sarcastically.)* Thank you, Yankel — is that what you want to hear? — thank you for leading me down the road to prostitution. I can't thank you enough.

JACK. Sara.

SARA. You took my soul — and threw it away.

JACK. We had no choice. Rivkele has a choice.

SARA. We had a choice. You had no faith.

JACK. Faith? The faith was beaten out of me. I had to survive. Things were gonna be different for her. Remember? That was what we wanted. That's what all these years have been about. No mixing between upstairs and downstairs! How many times have you heard me say that? They've gotta be kept separate, like kosher from *treyf*!

SARA. *(Ironically.)* Today was gonna be a new beginning, remember? *(He breaks down sobbing.)*

JACK. I'm sorry ...

SARA. Oh, Yankeleh ...

JACK. I didn't mean what I said.

SARA. No? Sounded to me like you meant exactly what you said.

JACK. I say things sometimes …

SARA. What, you say you're sorry and that makes everything all right?

JACK. What more can I say? Forgive me. Please. Please, Sara.

SARA. All right. *(A beat.)* I forgive you. God help me, but I do. *(Pause.)* Come. Let's go to bed. You'll talk to her in the morning. *(Helps him to his feet.)* Come, *tateleh. (As they exit, her arm around him:)*

JACK. I want her to have a better life.

SARA. I know, I know.

JACK. A respectable life.

SARA. Yes, yes … *(They exit to their bedroom. Rumble of thunder. Downstairs, Manke emerges from her cubicle in a camisole; her customer dresses and leaves. She goes to the window and inhales the rain-cleansed air. She climbs out of the window and stands in the rain under Rivkele's window.)*

MANKE. *(Whispers, calls.)* Rivkele! Rivkele! *(Rivkele hears her, goes to her window. Hindl remains in the shadows of the brothel, eavesdropping.)*

RIVKELE. Oh, Manke! It's you, it's you, thank God it's you!

MANKE. Have they gone to bed?

RIVKELE. I think so.

MANKE. Did he hurt you?

RIVKELE. No, but he scares me so much. It's all my fault: I went down to find you and Shloyme was there and —

MANKE. *(Overlap.)* Shhh shhh shhh. It's all right; it doesn't matter. Come down.

RIVKELE. What?!

MANKE. The rain feels wonderful! Come down right now!

RIVKELE. We'll get soaked!

MANKE. So what! Feel how warm the rain is!

RIVKELE. Oh, I would love to …

MANKE. Well, then do it!

RIVKELE. But what if my father…?

MANKE. The hell with him!

RIVKELE. *(Giggles.)* Manke!

MANKE. We'll dance to spring! *(Spins herself around a puddle.)*
RIVKELE. *(Torn, considering it.)* Oh … I don't know what to do …
MANKE. Rivkele …
RIVKELE. I can't. I mustn't.
MANKE. Stop saying that!
RIVKELE. What if he finds out?
MANKE. What if he does? We have nothing to lose! Our secret is out!
RIVKELE. Yes! You're right. Wait … *(She goes to her bed and props up her pillows to make it look like she's sleeping, then returns to the window.)* Oh, God … I can't believe I'm doing this … *(She climbs down the fire escape ladder in her bare feet.)*
MANKE. Yay!
RIVKELE. Ooo, it is warm!
MANKE. I told you! *(Manke takes Rivkele's hands and together they gaily swing around. Their laughter subsides. Manke strokes Rivkele's wet hair and face. Gently:)* Close your eyes. Feel it? Feel how nice that is?
RIVKELE. Mmm.
MANKE. Let the rain wash away your sadness. Doesn't that feel good?
RIVKELE. Oh, yes!
MANKE. And breathe it in. *(They inhale together.)* Do you smell how sweet it is?
RIVKELE. Yes!
MANKE. Who would think the city night could smell so sweet?
RIVKELE. Oh! My heart.
MANKE. What.
RIVKELE. Feel it. It's pounding. *(Manke puts her hands on Rivkele's chest.)*
MANKE. Ooo, yes. Your heart is pumping so fast. *(Silence as she slowly caresses Rivkele's breasts.)* Your skin is so cool under my hands … like cool white snow … *(Rivkele's teeth chatter.)* Oh, my darling, you're shivering. Come, let's go inside … *(As Manke helps Rivkele back inside, Hindl hides behind the drape of her cubicle and continues to listen. Manke sits Rivkele down on the sofa, gets a towel and a blanket.)*
RIVKELE. I feel so cold all of a sudden …

48

MANKE. *(Wrapping her in the blanket.)* Here ... *(Sits with her.)* Cuddle with me. That's right. Snuggle up close. Feel how warm I am?
RIVKELE. Oh, yes.
MANKE. You hold me, and I'll hold you. There. *(They do.)* Better?
RIVKELE. Oh, yes. I love how you hold me. No one ever holds me like this.
MANKE. Me, neither.
RIVKELE. No? But all those men ...
MANKE. Those men. *(A laughable notion.)* I feel nothing with them. Just when I'm with you. *(Rivkele strokes Manke's hand.)*
RIVKELE. I love your hands.
MANKE. *(Takes it away; self-conscious.)* I hate how they look.
RIVKELE. *(Takes them back.)* Oh, no, they're so long and sleek and warm. *(Manke strokes her own face with Rivkele's hair, inhaling its scent.)*
MANKE. Mmm ... Your hair smells so clean. Like the rain. So fresh, so soft. Let me fix your hair, like a bride. *(She begins to.)*
RIVKELE. Ooo, yes!
MANKE. You be the bride. A lovely young bride. And I'll be the bridegroom, your new husband. All right?
RIVKELE. Yes!
MANKE. The night of the wedding: The celebration is over. All the guests have gone home. We're sitting at the table with your mama and papa. And — wait! It's getting late. Your parents go off to bed. We're all alone. *(Rivkele mock-gasps.)* The nervous bride and her bridegroom. And I sit closer to you, as close as can be. And we hug. Like this. *(They hug.)* Ooo, yes! Tight, tight, as tight as can be. And I kiss you. Like this. *(She kisses Rivkele.)* And we blush, both of us. And we go to your bed, now our marriage bed, and we lie there, the two of us, side by side, and no one sees, no one knows, and no one cares, for we're married now, just a bride and her bridegroom, and we fall asleep in each other's arms, like this, *(Gets on top of her.)* forever and ever and ever ... *(Hindl comes out of her cubicle, feigning surprise at seeing them.)*
HINDL. Oops! Pardon me! *(Manke and Rivkele sit up, mortally embarrassed.)*
MANKE. Hindl! What are you doing sneaking up on us?

HINDL. I wasn't sneaking, I was coming out to look at the rain.

MANKE. The rain stopped. Go back to bed.

HINDL. Gee, I knew you girls were friendly, but …

MANKE. Mind your own business.

RIVKELE. Please don't tell my father. If he finds out I was down here …

HINDL. Boy, he's got some temper, doesn't he! I might just go upstairs right now …

RIVKELE. Don't! Please!

MANKE. Why don't you leave us alone?

HINDL. All right. I was gonna tell you something but if you don't want to hear it …

MANKE. What.

HINDL. *(Sing-song.)* Good ni-ight!

MANKE. Hindl! What.

HINDL. Okay, you twisted my arm. What if I told you … Jack was shutting down the business?

MANKE. He is not.

HINDL. Yes he is. You think I would lie about something like that?

RIVKELE. It's true; I heard him talking about it.

MANKE. When's this supposed to happen?

RIVKELE. Soon. After my wedding.

MANKE. Oh, God.

RIVKELE. It's good news, isn't it?

MANKE. No.

RIVKELE. Why?

HINDL. *(Overlap.)* What's so good about it? I mean, for you. Think about it, *mameleh:* If he shuts this place down where does that leave you and Manke?

RIVKELE. I'll still be upstairs and she'll still be downstairs.

MANKE. No …

HINDL. *(Overlap.)* Not if she's booted out and you're someone's little wife.

RIVKELE. Oh, God … I hadn't thought about that.

HINDL. You're not gonna be able to hop the fire escape and see her anymore.

RIVKELE. *(To Manke.)* What are we going to do?

MANKE. I don't know.

HINDL. Well, I know what *I'm* doing. I'm getting the hell out of here.

MANKE. And going where?

HINDL. Someplace new. Someplace safe. *(To Rivkele.)* That your father doesn't know from. Or your mother. Where there's no more hitting. No more yelling.

RIVKELE. Where is this place?

HINDL. Not far. A few blocks away. But it might as well be the moon.

MANKE. Okay, Hindl. What's the story?

HINDL. You wanna know the story? Shloyme's gonna marry me. That's the story.

MANKE. *(Over "That's ... ")* What does Shloyme have to do with this?

HINDL. He found us a place. Of our own. On Rivington Street. Plenty of room for everybody.

RIVKELE. For everybody?

HINDL. Yeah, for you, too, baby.

MANKE. Oh, I see ...

RIVKELE. What. I don't understand.

MANKE. She means a place like this. No way on earth would I take you to a place like this.

HINDL. You want to be together, don't you?

RIVKELE. Yes!

MANKE. But not like that. I would never do that to you. Never.

HINDL. So how you gonna be together? Huh? He'll do everything he can to keep you apart. You know he will.

RIVKELE. I'd die if I couldn't see you anymore ...

MANKE. This is no kind of life for someone like you. This is no life for anybody.

RIVKELE. And what kind of life am I looking at now?, living under my father's roof, married off to a man I haven't even met?! *(Cries.)* I want to be with you. I have to be with you ...

HINDL. All right, enough already, girls. Come, if we're gonna go, let's go. *(Hindl gets a suitcase and starts packing.)*

RIVKELE. You mean now?!

MANKE. *(Overlap.)* Tonight?!

HINDL. Yeah! I'm outta here tonight. You coming with me, or what?

RIVKELE. Let's do it! Let's have an adventure!

MANKE. An adventure?

RIVKELE. Yes! You and me!

HINDL. Thatta girl!

MANKE. *(To Rivkele.)* This is what you want?

RIVKELE. Yes.

HINDL. Okay! Let's get out of here.

RIVKELE. Wait! Like this? *(Meaning her attire.)* I can't go like this. I have to go back up.

HINDL. No, no, forget about your clothes.

RIVKELE. I just need to pack a few things.

HINDL. Too risky. What if your father hears you?

MANKE. She's right. Forget it.

HINDL. You'll wear *our* clothes.

RIVKELE. *Your* clothes?!

HINDL. Yeah! Let's see, what do we have for you … *(She goes through a rack of garments.)* Try this … *(She gives Rivkele a dress, which Rivkele puts on with pleasure.)*

RIVKELE. Ooo! I love it! It feels so silky.

HINDL. *(Applying lipstick.)* I'm not gonna miss this place, that's for sure. Not for one minute. *(She starts applying lipstick to Rivkele's mouth.)* Here, kid … Pucker up.

MANKE. No! No lipstick.

RIVKELE. No, I want to see … *(Hindl finishes applying the lipstick and takes Rivkele to a mirror.)*

HINDL. There! Now don't you look pretty!

RIVKELE. What do you think, Manke? You think I look pretty?

MANKE. *(Rueful.)* Yes. Very pretty.

HINDL. Here, try these shoes. Do they fit?

RIVKELE. *(Puts them on.)* Yes! Good enough!

HINDL. Good! Now: What you need is a hat! *(Hindl puts a hat on Rivkele's head. Rivkele admires herself in the mirror. Hindl wraps her boa around her with a flourish.)* Ladies and gentlemen … Miss Clara Bow! *(Rivkele and Hindl laugh. Manke does not. Their laughter subsides. Rivkele watches Manke pack in silence.)*

RIVKELE. Manke?

MANKE. *(Smiles.)* Come. We should go. *(She clicks shut her suitcase and slips her arm through Rivkele's. The three of them begin to exit.)*

HINDL. You won't be sorry. Things'll be different with Shloyme and me. I promise: a whole new world. Wait till he sees who I'm bringing home! *(Rivkele lingers to take a final look at her building. Manke takes her hand and they run off together. Lights shift. The dead of night. Upstairs: Jack, in a robe, unable to sleep, enters the living room. Restless, he pours himself some wine, sits, thinks. Downstairs: a shriek. Basha, wraithlike in her nightclothes, comes out of her cubicle in an agitated dream state.)*

BASHA. Mama?! Don't hurt me, you're hurting me...! *(Reyzl comes out of her cubicle, comforts Basha.)*

REYZL. Basha ... Shhh ... You're dreaming ...

BASHA. Please, Mama ... Stop!

REYZL. Wake up!

BASHA. *(Wakens.)* Oh, God ... It was my poor dead mama again ...

REYZL. I know.

BASHA. Howling and weeping ... Scratching my face, pulling my hair.

REYZL. Shhh ...

BASHA. *(Haunted voice.)* "For this I saved you? For this?" Oh, God, I've shamed her so ... *(She sobs in Reyzl's arms.)*

REYZL. Poor Basha. Try to sleep. Come, *mamaleh,* I'll tuck you back in. Shhh ... *(She leads Basha back to bed. Upstairs, Jack quietly enters Rivkele's room and approaches the cabinet housing the Torah. It seems to glow from within.)*

JACK. *(Whispers, to the scroll.)* Hello, God. It's me, Yankel Tshaptshovitsh. Welcome to my home. God, you see everything. You know everything I do. If you want to punish me, punish me. But the innocent girl who sleeps here — this angel — doesn't know the meaning of the word "sin." Have pity on her. Amen. *(Sits, whispers gently to the form lying in bed.)* Rivkele? I don't want to wake you. I just want to be near you. *(He pulls up a chair and sits.)* I used to sit by your cradle while you slept, just to listen to you breathe. I couldn't believe the perfect little miracle God gave to two sinners! You are not the work of a vengeful God, my darling. *(A beat.)* I had to find my way by myself, on the street. A greenhorn in America, a scrawny orphan. What did I have? I had nobody; I had nothing. Just my wits. But you, my precious, you're gonna have the life in America we only dreamed about. You, and your children, and their children. Yankel's children. You'll live the dream. *(A beat. More hurt than anger:)* So, when I find out you've been going downstairs when I told you never to go downstairs ... When I find out you're making friends with the wrong sort of people ... And lying to me! Sweetheart! Is it any wonder I get upset? I'm better now. I had a talk with your mother. I've calmed down. We'll talk in the morning. Everything will be all right. *(He reaches for "her" and is shocked to find pillows where he thought she lay. He flings off the blanket and shouts in horror.)* Oh, my God! NO!!!!! *(Jack storms out of the apartment and down the stairs. Upstairs: Sara runs out from the bedroom.)*

SARA. Jack? *(Discovers Rivkele is missing.)* Oh, my God ... *(Gets her shoes, puts on a coat.)*

JACK. *(Overlap.)* Rivkele?! *(Jack tears into the brothel, pulls Reyzl and Basha out of their beds. They're terrified.)* Where is she? Hm? Where is Rivkele? Is she here? Is she hiding?

REYZL. I don't know!

JACK. *(To Basha.)* Do you?

BASHA. No! *(He releases her, pulls open the drapes, exposing the empty cubicles. Upstairs, Sara takes cash from a jar, stuffs it in her purse.)*

JACK. Up! Everybody up! Manke! Hindl! *(He sees evidence of packing. It dawns on him.)* Oh, my God ... *(To the others.)* Where are they?! Where did they go!

REYZL. We don't know! We were sleeping! *(He storms out, encounters Sara on the stairs.)*

SARA. Did you find her? Is she down there?

JACK. No! She's gone! She went with them!

SARA. With who?

JACK. Manke's gone and so is Hindl! She ran away! Your precious daughter! She ran away! With those whores! *(He rampages around his living room, tossing furniture around, breaking glassware, etc. Sara goes to the girls.)*

BASHA. *(Frightened.)* What's happening?

SARA. God help us! I don't know.

BASHA. It's my mother's revenge!

SARA. Go find Reb Eli. Tell him something terrible has happened. Tell him we need his help. Can't have a wedding without a bride. Hurry! *(Reyzl and Basha don coats and go. Sara goes back upstairs to find Jack disconsolate and the apartment in shambles. She begins to pick up the pieces.)* Our daughter ran away, but must you destroy our home, too?

JACK. What difference does it make? It's all shit. *(A mournful wail.)* Rivkele!

SARA. Listen to you! So she's run away! What seventeen-year-old girl hasn't done that!

JACK. What can I do? There's nothing I can do!

SARA. Go out there! Go out on the street yourself! Ask around! Ask the scum you know who make their lives in the gutter! Ask *them* if they've seen your daughter!

JACK. I can't. I can't move my legs. It doesn't matter anymore. Nothing matters. God doesn't want it. He doesn't want it ...

SARA. God doesn't want it? *You're* the one who doesn't want it! *(She puts a coat on.)*

JACK. Where you going?

SARA. To the streets! If you want to sit here eating your *kishkes* out, fine! I'm going out to look for her! *(Sara goes downstairs and exits. Lights shift. Minutes pass. Just before dawn. Eli rushes up the street and finds Jack upstairs, sitting amid the wreckage.)*

ELI. *(Entering.)* Oh, my God! Look at you! Look at this place!

JACK. *(Muttering.)* Eli, Eli ... She's gone, Eli. My Rivkele. She left me.

ELI. Pull yourself together ...

JACK. She ran away with whores.

ELI. Quiet. Don't speak that way.

JACK. The marriage I wanted for her. The future. God doesn't want it.

ELI. Shhh!

JACK. *(Overlap.)* He doesn't want it. It isn't meant to be. *(Wails.)* Rivkele...! Rivkele...!

ELI. What is the matter with you?! You want the whole world to hear? Things like this are best kept private.

JACK. I don't care who hears. My daughter is gone. No more daughter. Rivkele! *(Breaks down sobbing.)*

ELI. Enough. You're acting like a crazy man.

JACK. I am crazy. Crazy to believe that my faith would not be

55

mocked. She's gone to the devil, I just know it.

ELI. Stop it. That isn't true.

JACK. Yes. I know what happens out there. She'll feel … temptation.

ELI. Yankel!

JACK. She will. And once it starts to grow inside her …

ELI. Uy uy uy.

JACK. *(Continuous.)* Once it starts, she won't know how to fight it. She'll surrender. Just like the rest of us sinners.

ELI. All right, now stop that right this minute.

JACK. If only she had died before her time …

ELI. What kind of nonsense is *that* now?!

JACK. If she had died, at least I would have known that I buried a pure child. But now…? *(Takes Jack by the hand into Rivkele's room, stands before the scroll.)*

ELI. Come. Let us pray!

JACK. What's the point? He doesn't hear me. He hasn't heard me all along.

ELI. Don't say that! Pray to Him! Pray for His forgiveness!

JACK. *(To the scroll.)* Show me! What kind of God are you?!

ELI. Yankel!

JACK. Perform a miracle! Go on! Send down a fire to consume me!

ELI. Enough!

JACK. *(Continuing.)* Open up the ground and let it swallow me up!

ELI. Enough with that!

JACK. Please please please, God, please protect my child. Send her back to me as pure, as innocent as she was. Otherwise I say that You are no God at all!

ELI. *(Aghast.)* You mustn't speak this way!

JACK. *(Continuing.)* You are vindictive! No better than a man!

ELI. That is blasphemy! Beg His forgiveness! Pray with me! Now! *(Eli leads Jack in prayer. Lights shift. Minutes pass. Sara hurries down the street with Shloyme.)*

SHLOYME. *(On the move.)* This better be good, dragging me out of my poker game …

SARA. What do *you* care, you were losing. Come, I'll give you some schnapps … *(She enters the brothel, pours drinks.)*

SHLOYME. *(Hesitates.)* Un-uh, no thanks, I don't want to see your husband.

SARA. Don't worry about him ... He's fast asleep.

SHLOYME. *(Enters.)* I liked him better before he found God.

SARA. *(Hands him a drink.)* You and me both. *L'khaim. (They drink.)* Got a cigarette? *(He gives her one, holds her hand as he lights it for her.)*

SHLOYME. You know? You must've been some looker.

SARA. Yeah? Well, you're right.

SHLOYME. Even now. You're not bad.

SARA. That's some compliment coming from you — seeing what taste in women you have. I mean, really, Shloyme: Hindl?

SHLOYME. Oh, come on, Hindl's not so bad.

SARA. No?! She's bounced around every flophouse on the Lower East Side, that girl! She's all used up! You — you're young, you're smart, you're not bad-looking ...

SHLOYME. Gee, thanks.

SARA. You could get any girl you want! A girl from a good family, even. Have a little self-respect! Don't sell yourself short!

SHLOYME. How come you're so interested in *me* all of a sudden?

SARA. I hate to see all that potential go to waste. *(She touches him. He considers it, then moves away.)*

SHLOYME. What'd you want to talk about anyway?

SARA. Business.

SHLOYME. Yeah? So talk. *(She takes cash out of her purse.)* What's all that?

SARA. Investment for the future. Three or four hundred — I'm not sure, I haven't counted it lately.

SHLOYME. What're you doing walking around with all that money?

SARA. You can have it — it's yours.

SHLOYME. What do you mean it's mine? How's it mine?

SARA. Just tell me where my daughter is.

SHLOYME. Your daughter?! How'm I supposed to know? *(During the above, Hindl runs up the street and enters the brothel.)*

HINDL. I did it, Shloym! I got you the girls! Just like I said. Manke and Rivkele, too!

SHLOYME. *(Comprehending.)* Oh ...

SARA. *(Overlap.)* Where is she?! Huh?! Where'd you take her?!

HINDL. Damned if I tell you!

SARA. Bitch! *(To Shloyme.)* Is opening a house with a broken-down whore the best you can dream about? Is it?

HINDL. *(Over "Is it?")* Screw you!

SARA. You can do anything. This is America. This'll help you get started.

HINDL. That Rivkele's a gold mine. That face, that little body of hers? The men are gonna be all over her — they're gonna be lining up! *(Sara thrusts the money at him.)*

SARA. Tell me where she is! What's the address?

HINDL. Don't do it. The girl's worth a lot more than a wad of cash. *(Sara takes off her earrings.)*

SARA. Take these, too. Hock 'em. That's hundreds right here. *(Shloyme is considering it.)*

HINDL. *(To Shloyme.)* Don't. We're so close! We're in business, baby. We're all set. We're getting married! Let's do it today!

SARA. *(Overlap.)* Here's your ticket, here it is, right here, right in my hand ...

HINDL. You love me! I know you love me! *(Shloyme and Hindl look at one another.)*

SHLOYME. *(While looking at Hindl.)* Two-eleven Rivington Street. *(He takes the jewelry. Hindl cries out. To Sara.)* Come, I'll walk you.

SARA. Thanks. *(Sara walks past Hindl who stands crumpled in the doorway.)*

SHLOYME. *(To Hindl.)* Hey. Let's face it: It's for the best. *(Hindl slaps his face. He and Sara exit down the street. Hindl, depressed, goes into her cubicle and draws the drape. Eli is pacing upstairs. Jack still sits despondently.)*

ELI. All is not lost. We can still save this match. When I talked to the boy's father, I dropped a few hints that the bride's family ... that maybe she doesn't come from the best of families and he didn't bat an eye. He still wants to meet you. I said I would bring him around first thing this morning.

JACK. This morning?! But how can he come?! There is no match! I have no daughter!

ELI. He doesn't have to meet the girl. He wants to meet you. We can buy some time. Now, please, get dressed and let's clean up this mess; we can't have it looking like this. *(Jack dresses while Eli picks up. Lights shift. Minutes pass. Morning. Sara comes down the street with her arm around Rivkele, who is wrapped in a large shawl.)*

SARA. Thank God I found you. You had yourself a misadventure, that's all. What child doesn't get into mischief every now and then?

RIVKELE. Where's Manke?

SARA. Forget about Manke. I don't think you'll be seeing Manke anymore. Now: When your father asks questions, don't say any more than you have to. Remember: The fewer words the better.

RIVKELE. Mama … *(At the steps, Sara fixes Rivkele's appearance.)*

SARA. Now, let's see … If only I had a comb. I'd fix your hair in braids.

RIVKELE. Leave it! I don't want my hair in braids!

SARA. *(Taken slightly aback.)* All right. We'll leave it.

RIVKELE. Please don't make me go up there.

SARA. He's not gonna hurt you. I promise. I won't let him.

RIVKELE. You always let him.

SARA. *(Taken further aback.)* Rivkele!

RIVKELE. It's all right, Mama, I know: We all take what we can get.

SARA. Hate me all you like …

RIVKELE. I don't hate you.

SARA. Hate your father. But don't — I beg you — don't destroy your future out of spite. This marriage …

RIVKELE. Mama …

SARA. It's a real opportunity! It's a way out! We can still make it happen! No one has to know anything! Come, sweetheart, whatever you do, don't make him mad. *(They go upstairs. Eli sees them approach from the top of the stairs.)*

ELI. Thank God! They're here!

JACK. *(Still dazed.)* What?

ELI. Your wife and child. See? God did help you. He punishes but He also heals. *(To Rivkele.)* Hello, dear. Thank God you're home safely. You had us all so worried there for a time. *(To Yankel.)* Now: Before anything else should go wrong, let me quick find the father of the bridegroom and finish the deal. And no hemming or hawing about the wedding, either.

JACK. *(To Rivkele, but not looking at her.)* I just want to know one thing. And I want the truth.

ELI. *(To Yankel.)* Leave it alone, Yankel. Just thank God for her return and leave it alone.

SARA. He's right, Yankel.

JACK. Just the truth. That's all I ask.

ELI. God will help and, in time, everything will work itself out. *Tshuvah, tefilah, tzedaka:* penitence, prayer, and charity. *(To Sara.)* You might want to tidy up a little bit.

SARA. Yes; I will.

ELI. And cheer up, everybody. Smile. You wouldn't want anyone to think something was wrong. I'll be back. *(Eli goes down the stairs, exits. Jack, Sara, and Rivkele stand in silence, the girl's face still obscured by her shawl. Jack approaches her. She flinches.)*

JACK. I only want to see your face. Let's see … *(He gently reveals her face; she averts her eyes.)* There you are, my darling. *(To Sara, hopefully.)* See? *(Sara nods.)* It's still the same girl. Isn't it?

SARA. Yes, it is.

JACK. *(To Rivkele.)* Come. Sit with me. *(Rivkele doesn't move.)* Don't be shy.

RIVKELE. I'm not shy.

JACK. Sit with me, I said.

RIVKELE. No, Papa.

JACK. No?

SARA. Your father wants you to sit with him.

RIVKELE. And I told him I don't want to. *(To Jack, defiantly.)* No, thank you. I'll stand.

JACK. *(To Sara.)* What kind of talk is this? She runs away from home and she comes back with a mouth?

RIVKELE. Not a mouth. Just a tongue.

JACK. Well! Well!

SARA. Yankel.

JACK. *(To Rivkele.)* I have only one question. Only one. But I want the truth. You understand?

RIVKELE. Papa …

JACK. Do you?

RIVKELE. I understand.

JACK. *(Pause; gently.)* Tell me you're the same girl who left here last night. Tell me you're the same, pure girl. That's all I want to hear. You can tell me, darling.

RIVKELE. I don't know!

JACK. You don't know?!

RIVKELE. What is "pure"? I don't know what it means!

JACK. That's ridiculous! Look me in the eye and tell me. Tell me the truth. *(Rivkele looks at him but doesn't say anything. Silence. He unravels her shawl, unveiling her garish dress.)* Oh, my God! *(Jack puts his fingers around her neck. Rivkele is not afraid.)*

SARA. Don't!

JACK. *(To Rivkele.)* If I had done this, long ago …

SARA. Jack!

JACK. *(Continuous, ignoring Sara.)* If I had twisted your neck off before you grew up …

SARA. Oh, my God, Jack …

JACK. If I had cut off your breath … Maybe we all would've been better off.

SARA. Stop it!

JACK. *(Tearfully.)* Look at you!

RIVKELE. Go ahead! Do it now! I don't care!

SARA. Rivkele! *(Pulls her away from Jack.)*

RIVKELE. *(Continuous, to Jack.)* Cut off my breath, just as you've been suffocating me all my life! *(Sara gasps.)*

JACK. What are you talking about, suffocating.

SARA. Leave it alone, leave it alone, Jack …

RIVKELE. *(Overlap.)* You kept me locked in my room!

JACK. Locked in your room?!

RIVKELE. You made me your prisoner!

JACK. Darling! I was protecting you!

RIVKELE. From what?

JACK. From evil! From sin! It's a sinful world out there! You're just a child!

RIVKELE. No! I'm not just a child! Not anymore!

JACK. *(A beat.)* What do you know?

RIVKELE. Everything! I know everything! *(Meanwhile, Eli and the prospective in-law, the father of the would-be bridegroom, come hurriedly down the street and mount the stairs.)*

ELI. *(Animatedly, while walking.)* Yes, yes, he's very eager to meet you. And his daughter! Such a fine girl, and a pretty one! A scholarly son-in-law he's after, and he'll support them the rest of their lives.

PROSPECTIVE IN-LAW. Ah, good, very good. *(They enter the*

apartment. Eli feels the chill in the air.)

ELI. Well! Here we are! Aren't we lucky! The entire Tshapshovitsh family … The mother of the bride …

PROSPECTIVE IN-LAW. How do you do?

SARA. How do you do.

ELI. The father of the bride …

PROSPECTIVE IN-LAW. *(To Yankel.)* Sir …

ELI. And the lovely Rivkele.

JACK. *(Bitterly.)* Yes, sir, a finer, chaste maiden you will never see.

ELI. Yes, well. *(To the in-law.)* Isn't she something? Can you imagine a better match for your boy?

JACK. *(Takes Rivkele's hand brusquely.)* Such a fine, chaste girl I have, no?

RIVKELE. Papa …

JACK. *(Maniacally.)* And what fine, chaste children she will have. *(To Sara.)* Right? Oh, what a future! What a bright future! All the years we dreamed of this … Her mother will lead her to the wedding canopy … in the whorehouse! *(Screams, shouts, cries: a cacophony.)*

PROSPECTIVE IN-LAW. What? What did he say?

ELI. *(Overlap.)* Oh, no, have you gone crazy?

JACK. Down to the whorehouse! Go! Get out of here, all of you!

RIVKELE. Papa! *(He pushes Rivkele toward the stairs.)*

JACK. You're all whores! *(To Sara, evicting her.)* You, too!

SARA. Jack! No!

JACK. Go! Everyone! Downstairs!

PROSPECTIVE IN-LAW. *(Overlap.)* What's going on here?

ELI. He's mad!

JACK. *(To Eli.)* You, too! Go on! Go! Goodbye!

ELI. You fool! You crazy fool!

JACK. Wait! Before you go … *(He rushes into Rivkele's room, takes the scroll.)*

ELI. Don't throw it all away! Think about what you're doing! *(Jack wields the Torah over his head, as if he is about to throw it at Eli.)* Remember God, Yankel! Remember God! *(Jack instead thrusts it into Eli's arms.)*

JACK. Take it with you! I don't need it anymore! *(Eli and the in-law leave with the scroll. Manke runs on and sees Rivkele, who breaks away from Sara and goes to her. Sara watches as the girls exit together,*

Manke holding Rivkele. Sara, shattered, goes back upstairs to join Jack in the ruins of their home. Downstairs, Hindl robotically applies lipstick before setting out for another day of walking the streets. Lights fade.)

End of Play

PROPERTY LIST

Vestment
Dishes
Food
Drinking glasses
Needle and thread (RIVKELE)
Lipstick (MANKE, HINDL)
Compact (MANKE)
Cigarettes and matches (MANKE, SHLOYME)
Basket (SARA, JACK)
Flowers (SARA)
Vase (SARA)
Paper flowers (RIVKELE)
Clothes (IRISH KID)
Sheet (BASHA)
Money (IRISH KID, SARA)
Billfold (JACK)
Makeup (BASHA, REYZL)
Ribbon-wrapped shawl (SHLOYME)
Baby Ruth (SHLOYME)
Tray (SARA)
Fork (HINDL)
Switchblade (JACK)
Schnapps (JACK, SARA)
Torah (SCRIBE, JACK)
Hair brush (RIVKELE)
Umbrellas (MANKE, CUSTOMER)
Bottle (JACK)
Pillows (RIVKELE)
Blanket (RIVKELE, MANKE)
Towel (MANKE)
Suitcase (HINDL, MANKE)
Wine (JACK)
Jar (SARA)
Purse (SARA)
Glassware (JACK)

SOUND EFFECTS

City sounds
Tin Pan Alley tune
Song
Creaking bedsprings
Rain
Thunder

NEW PLAYS

★ **THE CREDEAUX CANVAS by Keith Bunin.** A forged painting leads to tragedy among friends. "There is that moment between adolescence and middle age when being disaffected looks attractive. Witness the enduring appeal of Prince Hamlet, Jake Barnes and James Dean, on the stage, page and screen. Or, more immediately, take a look at the lithe young things in THE CREDEAUX CANVAS..." *–NY Times.* "THE CREDEAUX CANVAS is the third recent play about painters...it turned out to be the best of the lot, better even than most plays about non-painters." *–NY Magazine.* [2M, 2W] ISBN: 0-8222-1838-0

★ **THE DIARY OF ANNE FRANK by Frances Goodrich and Albert Hackett, newly adapted by Wendy Kesselman.** A transcendently powerful new adaptation in which Anne Frank emerges from history a living, lyrical, intensely gifted young girl. "Undeniably moving. It shatters the heart. The evening never lets us forget the inhuman darkness waiting to claim its incandescently human heroine." *–NY Times.* "A sensitive, stirring and thoroughly engaging new adaptation." *–NY Newsday.* "A powerful new version that moves the audience to gasps, then tears." *–A.P.* "One of the year's ten best." *– Time Magazine.* [5M, 5W, 3 extras] ISBN: 0-8222-1718-X

★ **THE BOOK OF LIZ by David Sedaris and Amy Sedaris.** Sister Elizabeth Donderstock makes the cheese balls that support her religious community, but feeling unappreciated among the Squeamish, she decides to try her luck in the outside world. "...[a] delightfully off-key, off-color hymn to clichés we all live by, whether we know it or not." *–NY Times.* "Good-natured, goofy and frequently hilarious..." *–NY Newsday.* "...[THE BOOK OF LIZ] may well be the world's first Amish picaresque...hilarious..." *–Village Voice.* [2M, 2W (doubling, flexible casting to 8M, 7W)] ISBN: 0-8222-1827-5

★ **JAR THE FLOOR by Cheryl L. West.** A quartet of black women spanning four generations makes up this hilarious and heartwarming dramatic comedy. "...a moving and hilarious account of a black family sparring in a Chicago suburb..." *–NY Magazine.* "...heart-to-heart confrontations and surprising revelations...first-rate..." *–NY Daily News.* "...unpretentious good feelings...bubble through West's loving and humorous play..." *–Star-Ledger.* "...one of the wisest plays I've seen in ages...[from] a master playwright." *–USA Today.* [5W] ISBN: 0-8222-1809-7

★ **THIEF RIVER by Lee Blessing.** Love between two men over decades is explored in this incisive portrait of coming to terms with who you are. "Mr. Blessing unspools the plot ingeniously, skipping back and forth in time as the details require...an absorbing evening." *–NY Times.* "...wistful and sweet-spirited..." *–Variety.* [6M] ISBN: 0-8222-1839-9

★ **THE BEGINNING OF AUGUST by Tom Donaghy.** When Jackie's wife abruptly and mysteriously leaves him and their infant daughter, a pungently comic reevaluation of suburban life ensues. "Donaghy holds a cracked mirror up to the contemporary American family, anatomizing its frailties and miscommunications in fractured language that can be both funny and poignant." *–The Philadelphia Inquirer.* "...[A] sharp, eccentric new comedy. Pungently funny...fresh and precise..." *–LA Times.* [3M, 2W] ISBN: 0-8222-1786-4

★ **OUTSTANDING MEN'S MONOLOGUES 2001–2002 and OUTSTANDING WOMEN'S MONOLOGUES 2001–2002 edited by Craig Pospisil.** Drawn exclusively from Dramatists Play Service publications, these collections for actors feature over fifty monologues each and include an enormous range of voices, subject matter and characters. MEN'S ISBN: 0-8222-1821-6 WOMEN'S ISBN: 0-8222-1822-4

DRAMATISTS PLAY SERVICE, INC.
440 Park Avenue South, New York, NY 10016 212-683-8960 Fax 212-213-1539
postmaster@dramatists.com www.dramatists.com

NEW PLAYS

★ **A LESSON BEFORE DYING by Romulus Linney, based on the novel by Ernest J. Gaines.** An innocent young man is condemned to death in backwoods Louisiana and must learn to die with dignity. "The story's wrenching power lies not in its outrage but in the almost inexplicable grace the characters must muster as their only resistance to being treated like lesser beings." —*The New Yorker.* "Irresistable momentum and a cathartic explosion…a powerful inevitability." —*NY Times.* [5M, 2W] ISBN: 0-8222-1785-6

★ **BOOM TOWN by Jeff Daniels.** A searing drama mixing small-town love, politics and the consequences of betrayal. "…a brutally honest, contemporary foray into classic themes, exploring what moves people to lie, cheat, love and dream. By BOOM TOWN's climactic end there are no secrets, only bare truth." —*Oakland Press.* "…some of the most electrifying writing Daniels has ever done…" —*Ann Arbor News.* [2M, 1W] ISBN: 0-8222-1760-0

★ **INCORRUPTIBLE by Michael Hollinger.** When a motley order of medieval monks learns their patron saint no longer works miracles, a larcenous, one-eyed minstrel shows them an outrageous new way to pay old debts. "A lightning-fast farce, rich in both verbal and physical humor." —*American Theatre.* "Everything fits snugly in this funny, endearing black comedy…an artful blend of the mock-formal and the anachronistically breezy…A piece of remarkably dexterous craftsmanship." —*Philadelphia Inquirer.* "A farcical romp, scintillating and irreverent." —*Philadelphia Weekly.* [5M, 3W] ISBN: 0-8222-1787-2

★ **CELLINI by John Patrick Shanley.** Chronicles the life of the original "Renaissance Man," Benvenuto Cellini, the sixteenth-century Italian sculptor and man-about-town. Adapted from the autobiography of Benvenuto Cellini, translated by J. Addington Symonds. "[Shanley] has created a convincing Cellini, not neglecting his dark side, and a trim, vigorous, fast-moving show." —*BackStage.* "Very entertaining…With brave purpose, the narrative undermines chronology before untangling it…touching and funny…" —*NY Times.* [7M, 2W (doubling)] ISBN: 0-8222-1808-9

★ **PRAYING FOR RAIN by Robert Vaughan.** Examines a burst of fatal violence and its aftermath in a suburban high school. "Thought provoking and compelling." —*Denver Post.* "Vaughan's powerful drama offers hope and possibilities." —*Theatre.com.* "[The play] doesn't put forth compact, tidy answers to the problem of youth violence. What it does offer is a compelling exploration of the forces that influence an individual's choices, and of the proverbial lifelines—be they familial, communal, religious or political—that tragically slacken when society gives in to apathy, fear and self-doubt…" —*Westword.* "…a symphony of anger…" —*Gazette Telegraph.* [4M, 3W] ISBN: 0-8222-1807-0

★ **GOD'S MAN IN TEXAS by David Rambo.** When a young pastor takes over one of the most prestigious Baptist churches from a rip-roaring old preacher-entrepreneur, all hell breaks loose. "…the pick of the litter of all the works at the Humana Festival…" —*Providence Journal.* "…a wealth of both drama and comedy in the struggle for power…" —*LA Times.* "…the first act is so funny…deepens in the second act into a sobering portrait of fear, hope and self-delusion…" —*Columbus Dispatch.* [3M] ISBN: 0-8222-1801-1

★ **JESUS HOPPED THE 'A' TRAIN by Stephen Adly Guirgis.** A probing, intense portrait of lives behind bars at Rikers Island. "…fire-breathing…whenever it appears that JESUS is settling into familiar territory, it slides right beneath expectations into another, fresher direction. It has the courage of its intellectual restlessness…[JESUS HOPPED THE 'A' TRAIN] has been written in flame." —*NY Times.* [4M, 1W] ISBN: 0-8222-1799-6

DRAMATISTS PLAY SERVICE, INC.
440 Park Avenue South, New York, NY 10016 212-683-8960 Fax 212-213-1539
postmaster@dramatists.com www.dramatists.com

NEW PLAYS

★ **THE CIDER HOUSE RULES, PARTS 1 & 2 by Peter Parnell, adapted from the novel by John Irving.** Spanning eight decades of American life, this adaptation from the Irving novel tells the story of Dr. Wilbur Larch, founder of the St. Cloud's, Maine orphanage and hospital, and of the complex father-son relationship he develops with the young orphan Homer Wells. "…luxurious digressions, confident pacing…an enterprise of scope and vigor…" *–NY Times.* "…The fact that I can't wait to see Part 2 only begins to suggest just how good it is…" *–NY Daily News.* "…engrossing…an odyssey that has only one major shortcoming: It comes to an end." *–Seattle Times.* "…outstanding…captures the humor, the humility…of Irving's 588-page novel…" *–Seattle Post-Intelligencer.* [9M, 10W, doubling, flexible casting] PART 1 ISBN: 0-8222-1725-2 PART 2 ISBN: 0-8222-1726-0

★ **TEN UNKNOWNS by Jon Robin Baitz.** An iconoclastic American painter in his seventies has his life turned upside down by an art dealer and his ex-boyfriend. "…breadth and complexity…a sweet and delicate harmony rises from the four cast members…Mr. Baitz is without peer among his contemporaries in creating dialogue that spontaneously conveys a character's social context and moral limitations…" *–NY Times.* "…darkly funny, brilliantly desperate comedy…TEN UNKNOWNS vibrates with vital voices." *–NY Post.* [3M, 1W] ISBN: 0-8222-1826-7

★ **BOOK OF DAYS by Lanford Wilson.** A small-town actress playing St. Joan struggles to expose a murder. "…[Wilson's] best work since *Fifth of July*…An intriguing, prismatic and thoroughly engrossing depiction of contemporary small-town life with a murder mystery at its core…a splendid evening of theater…" *–Variety.* "…fascinating…a densely populated, unpredictable little world." *–St. Louis Post-Dispatch.* [6M, 5W] ISBN: 0-8222-1767-8

★ **THE SYRINGA TREE by Pamela Gien.** Winner of the 2001 Obie Award. A breathtakingly beautiful tale of growing up white in apartheid South Africa. "Instantly engaging, exotic, complex, deeply shocking…a thoroughly persuasive transport to a time and a place…stun[s] with the power of a gut punch…" *–NY Times.* "Astonishing…affecting …[with] a dramatic and heartbreaking conclusion…A deceptive sweet simplicity haunts THE SYRINGA TREE…" *–A.P.* [1W (or flexible cast)] ISBN: 0-8222-1792-9

★ **COYOTE ON A FENCE by Bruce Graham.** An emotionally riveting look at capital punishment. "The language is as precise as it is profane, provoking both troubling thought and the occasional cheerful laugh…will change you a little before it lets go of you." *–Cincinnati CityBeat.* "…excellent theater in every way…" *–Philadelphia City Paper.* [3M, 1W] ISBN: 0-8222-1738-4

★ **THE PLAY ABOUT THE BABY by Edward Albee.** Concerns a young couple who have just had a baby and the strange turn of events that transpire when they are visited by an older man and woman. "An invaluable self-portrait of sorts from one of the few genuinely great living American dramatists…rockets into that special corner of theater heaven where words shoot off like fireworks into dazzling patterns and hues." *–NY Times.* "An exhilarating, wicked…emotional terrorism." *–NY Newsday.* [2M, 2W] ISBN: 0-8222-1814-3

★ **FORCE CONTINUUM by Kia Corthron.** Tensions among black and white police officers and the neighborhoods they serve form the backdrop of this discomfiting look at life in the inner city. "The creator of this intense…new play is a singular voice among American playwrights…exceptionally eloquent…" *–NY Times.* "…a rich subject and a wise attitude." *–NY Post.* [6M, 2W, 1 boy] ISBN: 0-8222-1817-8

DRAMATISTS PLAY SERVICE, INC.
440 Park Avenue South, New York, NY 10016 212-683-8960 Fax 212-213-1539
postmaster@dramatists.com www.dramatists.com